TRANSACTIONS

of the

American Philosophical Society

Held at Philadelphia for Promoting Useful Knowledge

VOLUME 82, Part 4, 1992

Changing Africa: The First Literary Generation of Independent Cape Verde

GERALD M. MOSER

THE AMERICAN PHILOSOPHICAL SOCIETY

Independence Square, Philadelphia

1992

Library of Congress Catalog
Card Number: 92-72961
International Standard Book Number 0-87169-824-2
US ISSN 0065-9746

TABLE OF CONTENTS

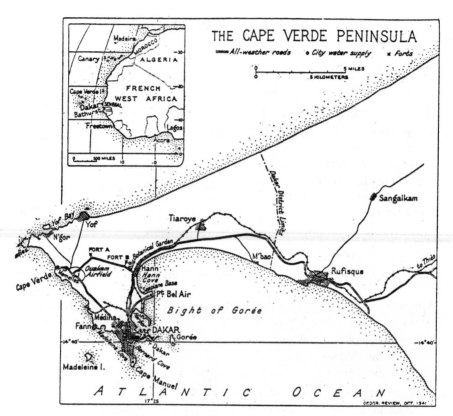

The Cape Verde Peninsula. Based on the 1:100,000 map of the Service Géographique de l'Afrique Occidentale Française à Dakar, 1928.

ACKNOWLEDGMENTS

I am indebted to Teobaldo Virgínio de Melo for information about several Cape Verdean writers and for help with Cape Verdean Creole, to Senhora Ivone Aída Ramos, J.L. Hopffer C. Almada, and A. Semedo for useful information, to Russell Hamilton for factual and stylistic suggestions, to Don Burness for improvements in the English translations of poetry, and to Inge Moser, my wife, for reading the entire manuscript with a critical eye.

To the American Philosophical Society I am most obliged since it provided a grant for the fieldwork on the Cape Verde Islands on which this work is based.

G.M.

UNIQUE ISLANDERS

There had been—and perhaps still exists—considerable curiosity about the further development of arts and letters in Africa since the last European colonies on that continent attained independence between 1974 and 75, following the virtually bloodless "Revolution of Carnations" in Lisbon. Under somewhat different circumstances, other parts of Africa, such as Senegal or Nigeria, had experienced the rise of indigenous literatures, which were to boast of writers known now all over the world, Senghor and Sembène, Achebe and Soyinka. Did the former Portuguese colonies bring forth a similar flowering after the removal of European tutelage, aggravated in their case by a fascistic police regime imposed from 1926 on? And if so, could one see an underlying general law that had been at work elsewhere, e.g., in the Americas, upon the rise of its independent nation states? Emerson's statement, made in his address "The American Scholar" (1837), which called for the literary emancipation of the young United States, might yet apply: "Our long apprenticeship to the learning of other lands draws to a close. [. . .] Events, actions arise that must be sung, that will sing themselves. [. . .] The literature of the poor, the meaning of household life, are the topics of the time. [. . .] Give *me* insight into today, and *you* may have the antique and the future worlds."

New nations are laboratories of new literatures. One such laboratory exists in an unlikely place, among a partly African partly European people, almost half of whom, if one includes their descendants, live in the United States practically unnoticed, except in certain coastal communities of southern New England, especially in and around Boston and Providence. They were known as the "Black Portuguese" or "Bravas" because they once used to set sail from the small island of Brava. That laboratory is the Cape Verde Islands. Those ten small volcanic specks of land lie in the South Atlantic, hundreds of miles distant from the African continent. On their rocky soil, poor in natural resources, ravaged periodically by droughts brought from the Sahel edge of the Sahara by an easterly wind, the Harmattan, the Islanders eke out a meager subsistence, survive and multiply. It seems incredible that this poorhouse of a nation, preoccupied with gathering its daily sustenance of corn, beans and fish, should find time or feel inclined to produce any art or literature. And yet the Islanders do.

One has to keep in mind that most Cape Verdeans are rural folk, have four years of schooling if they are fortunate, and lack the means to buy amenities such as toys or extra clothing, let alone newspapers and books. Visitors cannot help being amazed at their tenacity, their resilience, their

1

apparent gentleness. Why do they not despair? To be sure, centuries of hardship have produced fatalism and resignation that inspire certain *mornas*, songs that accompany the slow dance of the same name. But the Islanders do not quite give up, remaining intensely loyal to their native isle, always hoping for a good year, concretely visualized as the advent of a season of abundant rain, *aságua* (*as águas*, the waters).

On the poor soil of Cape Verde, Europe, in the person of the seafaring, trading Portuguese, entered into close relations with Black Africa, represented by enslaved men, women and children it carried there from the nearest mainland. Over five hundred years ago, the Portuguese built the first western-style city on Santiago, the largest island, complete with a hospital, a pillory, a fortress, a port, churches, monasteries, schools. From these beginnings sprang a free people, different from any other in Africa, with its own language, *Crioulo*, the daughter of pidgin Portuguese, related to the Creoles spoken in the towns of Guinea-Bissau and on the Islands of São Tomé e Príncipe.

From the middle of the nineteenth century on, works of fiction and poetry were written in Cape Verde and appeared in print, beginning with a novel, *O escravo* ("The Slave") in 1856. However, until the period between the two World Wars, this incipient literature remained a regional or colonial variant of the literature of Portugal. The foundations for a national literature were laid between 1935 and 1960. At that time, a small group of intellectuals gathered around the poet Jorge Barbosa in Mindelo, the principal harbor of the Islands. Inspired by the example of contemporary Brazilian writers, many of whom came from a similarly dry, impoverished region, the northeastern Hump of South America, they began to evolve specifically Cape Verdean writing by closely observing the speech, traditions and way of life of the common folk of the Islands. In 1936 they started a literary magazine, which they named *Claridade*— "Clarity" or "Brightness"—following precedents set, not in Portugal, but in France and the Americas. The irregularity of its publication until 1960 reflected the difficulty of Cape Verdean life. But the group's pioneering essays, studies, poetry and stories left a lasting mark. That became evident in November 1986 when the fiftieth anniversary of *Claridade* was commemorated in Mindelo by an international congress of writers and literary scholars under the auspices of the Cape Verdean government. The congress brought together three or four generations of Cape Verdean writers, including the youngest, coming to the fore since Independence, that is, since 1975.

The absence of partisanship during the sessions, or putting it positively, the spirit of friendly cooperation, was most remarkable. It was what Cape Verdeans call *junta-mon*, a joining of hands across generations, from the survivors of the initial *Claridade* circle to young writers and artists of the recently formed *Pró-Cultura* movement.

THE INDEPENDENCE GENERATION

At the *Claridade* congress of 1986 I had the good fortune to make the acquaintance of José Luís Hopffer C. Almada, a young man who turned out to be the leading spirit of *Pró-Cultura*. *Pró-Cultura* is the movement which had taken shape among those whom he calls the *Geração Mirabílica*; the Generation of the remarkable [year 1986] whom I propose to call the Independence Generation, composed of individuals born between 1950 and 1965. They were in their formative years when the Cape Verde Islands became politically independent. José Luís is from Santiago Island, where Praia, the capital, is situated, and it was there, too, that the movement had its origin. Praia has remained its center. José Luís is well connected, belonging as he does to the family of the present Minister of Culture, David Hopffer Almada. He asked me if I would be interested in meeting other members—artists and writers—and mentioned that they had started a cultural supplement of the principal newspaper, *Voz di Povo* ("The People's Voice"), as recently as the previous month of March (1986). It had been named *Voz di Letra*, "The Voice of Letters." Illustrating the difficulties of island existence, he explained that after the first five issues had appeared, further publication had to be postponed because of newsprint and power shortages.

My curiosity was increased when José Luís mentioned that the Movement had plans that seemed very ambitious under the circumstances: an independent literary magazine, an anthology of no fewer than fifty young Cape Verdean poets, and a theater group. From what he told me, but also from the art show and the concert which formed part of the Congress program, it seemed that the fine arts and belles lettres were very much alive. Nineteen eighty-six was indeed a remarkable year of cultural activity.

The following day brought another opportunity for chatting with José Luís while both of us were among the audience that waited for another young Cape Verdean to produce his translation of a new play by the Argentinean Manuel Puig. (Alas, the performance was abruptly stopped during the first scene by the angry director.) I learned that José Luís had recently returned from six years of studying at the universities of Berlin and Leipzig in East Germany. He added that he loved Leipzig and would gladly return there to continue his studies. He showed me two poems he had written there, one of them in German about a peace demonstration that had been forcibly stopped by the police. I would not have expected that some young Cape Verdeans had gone to Germany. Most who study abroad, traditionally do so in Portugal or France. Second, it was revealing that the former did not swallow official propaganda of the

3

East German Communists but kept a critical perspective on what they observed. And third, it was obvious that the prolonged stay in a foreign country had had a stimulating effect. Probably the exposure to the cultural life in a German city well known as a center of university research, music, and publishing had impelled this Cape Verdean to take bold initiatives in his own country.

José Luís must have been born about 1965. He had been a schoolboy, ten years of age, when Cape Verde became a nation state. Now in his twenties, his writing career had barely begun. Like the rest of the *Pró-Cultura* group he thus belonged to the first generation which could create in a society free from Portuguese tutelage and censorship. Supposing that they agreed with their government's plans, they could help with the building or "reconstruction," to use the terminology of the socialist state, turning Cape Verde toward the direction of Africa, away from Western Europe or the Americas. It remained to be seen whether that supposition was correct.

Having checked the dates when many of Hopffer Almada's writing contemporaries were born, I arrived at a working definition of them as a generation. Even so I had to base it on two somewhat arbitrary assumptions: 1) To belong to a particular generation, a span of fifteen years would be best between the oldest and the youngest members. 2) The oldest would have to have been in their mid-twenties when the Islands were granted independence in 1975, as far as this particular generation was concerned. Consequently, the Independence Generation would consist of people born between 1950 and 1965. Members of the Generation used to refer to it as "the Youngest Generation," *a Novíssima Geração*. That term is outdated already. Hopffer Almada sometimes also used the term "Generation of (19)80." It is appropriate, I believe, to characterize it by the political event that has determined their outlook on the world.

A related circumstance has influenced this generation: the concentration of artists, writers, and the more highly educated people generally in the capital city of Praia, where administrative positions are available and cultural institutions exist, such as the official *Instituto do Livro e do Disco* ("The Book and Record Institute") with its facilities for publication and distribution.

Two further traits distinguish the Independence Generation. Both relate to literature. One is the spontaneous nature of its *Pró-Cultura* movement, created before the government sponsored a national writers' union, the *Associação dos Escritores Caboverdianos*, following the example of Angola and Mozambique. *Pró-Cultura* was free to encourage independence and diversity. The other trait is the launching of its idealism, translated into action through *Fragmentos*, its own journal, in 1987, without reliance on official subsidies. In the past, periodicals had similarly served successive groups as rallying points and as outlets for short writings and black-and-white art work. As a result, historians use terms such as the *Claridade* Generation(s), the *Certeza* Generation, the *Ariope* Generation, and so forth when discussing twentieth-century literature.

Before examining the Independence Generation more closely, I had expected that it would exhibit characteristics which would accentuate the country's independence from Portugal: a preference for using the Creole language rather than Portuguese; a return to African roots; seeking inspiration in folk "orature," that is, in songs, stories and sayings; and last but not the least, a wholehearted acceptance of the dominant political system and ideology leading to a politically and socially committed production of art and literature.

In 1989 I had a chance to return to the Islands and spend a week in Praia. On short notice, friends enabled me to meet representatives of the younger set of writers, to find out what writing meant to them, and to acquire their books and periodicals on the spot. I am grateful to these friends, all of them Cape Verdeans, among them José Luís Hopffer C. Almada, Customs Director Arnaldo França, himself a writer and once editor of *Raízes*, a good literary journal, Jorge Miranda Alfama and Oswaldo Osório, respectively the director and bookstore manager of the *Instituto Nacional do Livro e do Disco*, Manuel Veiga, Director of the Office for Cape Verde's Historic Patrimony, and the poet Alexandre Semedo, editor of *Seiva*, the journal of JAAC-CV (*Juventude Africana Amílcar Cabral– Cabo Verde*), the official youth organization.

One week is too short a time to get to know everything about a literature that is in the process of becoming. Even so, I shall attempt to give an idea of the program(s) of this Independence Generation, its members, and the nature and quality of the work they have produced so far. My observations are the result of conversations, discussions, and readings.

THE *PRÓ-CULTURA* GROUP
WITHIN THE INDEPENDENCE GENERATION

Praia, the capital of the young Republic of Cape Verde, is a small town. To find one's way in it is easy. The various branches of government, as well as most business activities, cluster within the few blocks of the old part, on the level height locally referred to as the *Plateau*. It overlooks the port and the open sea on one side. On the other it dominates the populous districts on the plain below, called the *Achada*, seen against the backdrop of the denuded brown ridges of the *Serra dos Órgãos*, the "Organ Mountains," above which towers the cone of the *Pico d'Antónia*, "Antonia's Peak."

The town offers a neat, airy appearance. Its population treats the stranger most courteously—neither the few beggars nor the street vendors harass him. Everything proceeds in the leisurely fashion one has to adopt in the tropics. City life pulsates around two squares separated by a couple of blocks, the colorful and noisy open air market, where the townspeople buy their foodstuffs directly from the country folk, and the main *praça*, bounded by solid buildings—the state bank, the supreme court, the central administration and the cathedral, a very humble and prosaic edifice in comparison to the other buildings. None of them dates farther back than the early years of the past century. A small park occupies the middle of the *praça*. Its precious greenery and many benches attract the younger set among the citizens until late into the night. A café kiosk also acts as a magnet. The weather favors outdoors living. It had not rained in Praia for almost six months when I revisited the town at the end of March 1989.

At the northern end of the *Plateau* stands the *Liceu Domingos Ramos*, one of the few secondary schools serving the Islands. Its students will from time to time take the initiative to produce one or two issues of some little magazine. Next to the school one finds the prime minister's residence. Halfway between those two and the market is another government building, identified by the sign *Ministério de Turismo*. The house beside it harbors the headquarters of the national youth organization, where I bumped into the second writer belonging to the Independence Generation, Alexandre Semedo.

At least three bookstores were in the neighborhood: a Catholic one, another in close proximity to the first, kept by the Adventists, and the largest of the three, the brand new, well stocked store of the *Instituto do Livro Caboverdiano*, which had no fewer than two dozen recently published works by Cape Verdean authors for sale among its many books and periodicals. What a surprise! Still closer to the market were the

6

editorial offices of *Tribuna*, one of the three official journals of Praia, the other two being the daily *Voz di Povo* and the monthly *Seiva* ("Lifeblood").

Such was the environment in which José Luís Hopffer C. Almada had started *Pró-Cultura*. How far, I wondered, had his plans for it advanced since I had heard him talk about them more than two years earlier? Of the four projects he had sketched summarily during the conversations in 1986, one had become a reality, the second was ready for publication but delayed, the third remained in a nebulous state, and the fourth apparently had been given up. On the Islands, it requires unusual persistence to overcome ingrained habits, the narrow scope of the economy, the weak civic spirit, the debilitating hot and dry climate.

The dream of starting a review was fulfilled when the first issue of *Fragmentos* appeared in August 1987. As the editor, José Luís was seconded by an array of directors, advisory secretaries and graphic artists. It came out in a large size format, printed on excellent paper, with an abundance of illustrations, some of them resuscitating the *style nouveau* of all things, and it ran to over fifty pages. Obviously, *Pró-Cultura* wanted to make an impression. How could the young men and women afford such luxury? It turned out that they had persuaded private business firms to make funds available, a method new to Cape Verde. Even so, it threatened to become a short-lived venture, like all of its predecessors. The second issue had to be delayed until March 1988, while the combined third and fourth, of December, were followed by silence. The silence was broken in November 1989 with a double issue of 96 pages.

At the outset, a great deal of enthusiasm must have been engendered in *Pró-Cultura* circles: for in short course, other periodical publications made their appearance. Already in November 1986, at the time of the *Claridade* Symposium, another *Pró-Cultura*–related newspaper supplement, *Sopinha do Alfabeto* ("Nice Alphabet Soup") appeared suddenly and vanished as suddenly, in addition to the supplement of *Voz di Povo*, started also in 1986 by *Pró-Cultura* people under the guidance of two slightly older editors, Ondina Ferreira, born in 1948, and Oswaldo Osório, born in 1937. At the same time, *Seiva* started as the organ of the national youth organization and soon added *Estros da Seiva* ("Stirrings of Lifeblood"), a literary page by and for young people. The page was edited by Daniel Spínola, one of José Luís's assistants. In an editorial of No. 6 (December 1987), he stated that *Estros da Seiva* "was open to all young people, militant or not, to help build our common homeland, the one dreamed of by Amílcar Cabral." Half a year later, in March 1988, the glossy review *Magma* "erupted" on Fogo Island in São Filipe, the third largest town of Cape Verde. However, only a few of its contributors belonged to the Independence Generation. Besides, it limited itself to local subject matter, and it enjoyed official support. There were stirrings on Sal Island, where the international airport of the Islands is located and where Jorge Barbosa, Cape Verde's best poet of the mid-twentieth century, used to live: five young writers published their poems and stories collectively in 1987, and in 1989 a review, *Djâr d'Sal* ("Sal Island") made its debut.

The second project, probably closest to the hearts of the *Pró-Cultura* membership, was to be a comprehensive anthology that would give many young poets their first chance to see their writings published in book-form. José Luís had conceived the idea in March 1986. By autumn of the following year he had gathered some 300 poems from more than fifty aspiring authors. He named his anthology *Mirabilis* and wrote in its preface that theirs constituted a *geração mirabílica*, as amazing as the *welwitschia mirabilis* of the coastal desert in southern Angola, a plant which ordinarily looks like a beached octopus but springs to gigantic life as soon as it receives some moisture. Then it develops a large blossom and— thorns. He added: "Fortunately, we poets are likewise as stubborn as our environment."

These post-Independence poets had no single common outlook. Therefore, the anthology was to reflect the diversity of their tendencies, of their ages—ranging from eighteen-year old Mark D. Velhinho Rodrigues to fifty-six-year old João Rodrigues, and of their preferred language, whether standard Portuguese (the majority), Cape Verdean Creole (several), French (three poets) or English (one). It was to encompass the first fruits of their poetic inspiration in 1974 as well as their mature writings of the 1980s. The motto could have been "Diversity Enriches." As for diversity, José Luís had declared to Alexandre Semedo that diversity was a Cape Verdean characteristic and that he himself had no style of his own but was moving simultaneously along several paths. "I try to construct myself as a plural being in my Cape Verdean and universal way," he said to his interviewer (*Seiva*, no. 8, January 1989, p. 13). Such conscious multiplicity could point to illustrious precedents in the poetry of the Spaniard Antonio Machado and the Portuguese Fernando Pessoa.

The preface for *Mirabilis* ends with further programmatic statements. They refute one of my assumptions about the young writers. José Luís wrote that no "pamphletary texts" were admitted entrance into the anthology, whereas political "pamphleteering" had still prevailed during the transitional period that followed Independence. The changing social reality, he continued, required a new, different treatment of the old themes of love, work, social inequalities, Christian beliefs, the "incongruities" of daily living, etc. When we had met in Mindelo in 1986, he had already declared that *Pró-Cultura* rejected politically motivated pamphleteering and talking down to the people. One should listen to the people. Then one might learn something from them. After that one could try to raise their tastes. Not limiting itself to the local or Cape Verdean condition, however, poetry would express the total or universal human reality. It was significant that he quoted the great Jorge de Sena in this connection; for Sena has been a thoroughly individualistic and humanistic, though fiercely Portuguese poet of our time. A further surprise was the omission of Africa from José Luís's list of themes, perhaps because it was too obvious to have to be mentioned. On the other hand, he dropped a hint that was bound to puzzle the outsider. Certain themes, he wrote, had become taboo. Was he referring to fatalism, famine, drought or something else?

In the context of the preface one reminder looks like a protest: The Cape Verdean constitution guarantees freedom of literary creation. Yet, José Luís's reminder merely echoed what no lesser authority than Aristides Pereira, President of the Republic of Cape Verde, had said in 1986. At the end of the speech with which he opened the *Claridade* Congress, Pereira adroitly combined the idea of creative freedom with that of social responsibility:

What the intellectuals are expected to do is to serve our national liberation with their talent and creativity, by contributing their share to the forging of a mentality that will transform society radically from a humanistic perspective, so that greater justice and social progress will be accomplished. For this undertaking the freedom of artistic creation is fundamental. [. . .]

We appeal to the writers, the artists and, most of all, to the young intellectuals to seek new forms of cultural expression [. . .] by exercising their activity *with a complete freedom.*

One may be tempted to see a trace of the *glasnost* spirit in those words. They sounded so different from the view expressed six years earlier by another high official, Manuel Duarte, as to the role to be assigned to writers. Duarte regretted in his "Brief Notes on Cape Verdean Literature," to find manifestations of radical criticism or disillusionment in recent Cape Verdean poetry. He hoped to see committed writers "descend directly into the arena of daily reality" and "in a futuristic frame of mind announce the advent of the New Man, liberated at last in a transformed society." The "Notes," which did not contain any mention of creative freedom, were featured as the lead article of *Raízes*, no. 21, June 1984, the final issue of that review.

One of the older participants in the *Pró-Cultura* venture, Oliveira Barros, had written in no. 4 (1977) of the same review *Raízes* that the concept of an official, and in his words "idolatrous" culture would be bound to lead to repetitiveness, redundancy, empty rhetoric and glorification of the past. Such a culture would be totally ineffective for the purpose of transforming class society ("Six Theses on Cultural Resistance," pp. 66–67). Under a similar title ("Six Theses on the Freedom to Create"), a certain "Tuna Furtado"—no other than José Luís—took up Oliveira Barros's theme in the second issue of *Fragmentos*. In the same issue, an editorial claimed that *Pró-Cultura* pursued four aims:

- to create a communion of hope, production and ideas among young writers;
- to further artistic and cultural creation;
- to encourage tolerance, cooperation and criticism among *all* creators;
- and to propagate the new voices and values, thus furthering freedom of creation.

An essay by José Vicente Lopes, "Intellectual and Intellectuals," published in *Fragmentos*, no. 3/4 (1988), went one step further. Invoking and quoting President Pereira's appeal of 1986, Lopes condemned the authori-

tarian character of most African states because they discouraged intellectual activities, while observing "a civic silence" in Cape Verde "that
neither approves nor disapproves anything." He concluded that the
reason for such silence must be sought in the State being the principal
employer so that people had to be on the most cordial relations possible
with it, their "boss," in order to be able to get the milk the children at
home needed for their survival.

José Luís became similarly frank in the interview he gave Semedo.
Asked what he thought of the breaking of taboos, the discarding of stereo-
types and the much talked-about freedom of expression, he replied
emphatically:

Freedom of expression is the *sine qua non* of human citizenship. Without it, no
democracy! [. . .] The gradual humanization of the conditions under which man
exists, that is the goal. [. . .] Poetry and the poet are incompatible with any organic
(systematic?), administrative or political-ideological manipulation—*dirigismo*,
was his word—[. . .] Poetry is anti-totalitarian by definition (*Seiva*, no. 8, p. 14).

José Luís's third and fourth objectives for *Pró-Cultura* were hindered by
the same problems that beset *Fragmentos* and delayed the publication of
the anthology. As a movement, *Pró-Cultura* remained shapeless and
weak; it did not reach the stage of organization capable of helping
writers. The fourth project, a theater section, had been the most difficult
of all to achieve; for the Islands lack a tradition of institutions sustaining
a theater. Some attempts were made, but the only durable spectacle
seems to be the popular *carnaval*, and that only in a couple of places, such
as the town of Mindelo.

José Luís recalled the four principles that had inspired the founding
of the movement and its review two years earlier, restating them more
briefly, although a little grandiloquently:

a) The need to affirm the independent, autonomous nature of art being created
   and managed by its creators themselves;
b) The indispensable [freedom] to encourage aesthetic pluralism and literary/
   artistic dialogue or debate through methods exclusively based on aesthetic
   ideology and science;
c) The immediate development of an aesthetically innovative, humanistic, no
   longer alienated, universalist art with profound roots in the Cape Verdean
   essence;
d) The urgency of creating a modern tool for the affirmation of the Mirabilis
   Generation and the expression of all voices telling of a new approach to Cape
   Verdean society.

To these he now added a fifth principle:

e) The commitment to discover the forgotten or unpublished works and pages
   of our older men and women of letters, at the same time as the intention to
   explore the untrodden paths of our history and culture, and the rediscovery
   of our orature (Editorial, *Fragmentos*, nos. 5/6, November 1989, p. 3).

Pró-Cultura aimed at being the movement of the first generation following Independence. What attitude did it take toward the preceding generations? To gain its place in the sun did it attack them? The answer was foreshadowed in another organ of the Independence Generation, *Ponto & Vírgula* ("Period & Comma," that is, "Semicolon"), which Leão Lopes, a man of high idealism and bold initiative, edited with Germano Almeida in Mindelo from 1983 on until he ran out of funds in 1986. *Ponto & Vírgula* opened its columns wide to writers of all generations, from the *Claridade* group to the most recent. As a common enterprise it proposed "to stop and rethink our culture, our way of life, our identity, our existence in the world" (unsigned editorial, no. 1, February/March 1983). It published a special issue featuring the generally beloved educator and story writer António Aurélio Gonçalves, one of the *Claridade* pioneers of a literature dealing with the lives of humble Cape Verdeans. Leão Lopes's magazine in turn merely followed in the footsteps of the editor of *Raízes*, who from 1977 on had made quality of writing its criterion, barring no Cape Verdean of the past or present, as long as he cared for his Islands. Neither periodical let itself be made the vehicle of polemics by which some uncompromising authors attacked the *Claridade* group as "escapists" and "regionalists" because the group was unwilling to abandon the use of standard Portuguese and create a purely African literature.

Pró-Cultura dwelt on the continuity in Cape Verdean literature, particularly its poetry, "since all Cape Verdean generations belong to *Modernismo* since 1936," as Hopffer Almada expressed it in his interview with Semedo. He had already defined the position of his Movement in *Do convívio entre as gerações* ("On Conviviality Among Generations"), an article that appeared in the first issue of *Fragmentos*. He began by pointing out the example set by the *Claridade* group when the ninth issue of its review (1960) contained contributions by *four* different generations. In a resigned mood he concluded that his own *novíssima geração*, the youngest, was still feeling close to *Claridade* because Cape Verdean writers were "condemned to conviviality"—coexistence might be a better English term for it—as physical and economic conditions enforced scarcity of literary creation. Undeniably, there had been a break as far as politics and society were concerned. He dated it from Kaoberdiano Dambará's *Noti* ("Night," 1964), a book of poems in Creole, whose author "fully assumed the black component of our Cape Verdean people and identified himself completely with the oppressed." That radical position was shared by what he called the Generation of 1950, made up of poets—Dambará, Aguinaldo Fonseca, Gabriel Mariano and Ovídio Martins. They had not prevailed.

Visible signs of respect for earlier generations on the part of *Pró-Cultura* were homages, e.g., to the historian António Carreira (*Fragmentos* 3/4) and the poet Jorge Barbosa (*Fragmentos*, no. 1), of whom it wrote: "We pay him a symbolical homage extending to the *Claridade* movement as a whole."

When a meeting with six of the younger writers was arranged by Dr. Arnaldo França in the afternoon of 29 March 1989, as a roundtable discussion between them and two American visitors, Prof. Russell

Hamilton of Vanderbilt University and myself, I raised the question of what writers had influenced them and by implication what they thought of earlier generations. Those present—José Luís, José Vicente Lopes, Fernando Monteiro, José Maria Varela, Valdemar Velhinho Rodrigues and Jorge Tolentino—answered that Jorge Barbosa's poetry continued to exert an influence. Two more recent writers, Arménio Vieira and Corsino Fortes, attracted them more, however, because of their innovations, such as the symbols created by Fortes. A third poet of the same generation preceding Independence, João Varela, interested them, but to a lesser degree, as did Oswaldo Osório, who had tapped a hitherto unnoticed part of folklore, the work song. They liked the militant Creole poetry of Emanuel Braga Tavares, which they found more vigorous than Dambará's. Within their own age group, they felt drawn to the surrealism of Carlos Fonseca and to the work of Tomé Varela da Silva, who in their eyes had the merit of collecting folktales and, with A. Semedo's help, the songs of two popular women singers from the Santiago countryside.

Just as revealing were the omissions. No woman writer was mentioned, except Fátima Monteiro, and she only in passing (Monteiro lives in Somerville, Massachusetts). No prose writers, not even A.A. Gonçalves or Baltasar Lopes, the patriarch of Cape Verdean letters, whose death occurred later on during the same year. Were there no foreign influences? "Few," they replied. They added that it was difficult to obtain books from abroad.

What about the satirical vein I thought I detected in recent writing? Their only comment on this question was that one could not run away from social problems.

Indirectly, what had been said confirmed at least one of my initial assumptions. The new generation remained interested in the study of Cape Verdean folk literature.

SEVEN AUTHORS WHO BELONG TO
THE INDEPENDENCE GENERATION

An entire literary generation cannot be determined exclusively by the circumstances under which it arises or the aims it proclaims. Its character is shaped by the individuals that compose it. The idea was given lapidary expression by the Spanish philosopher Ortega y Gasset in one sentence: *Yo soy yo y mi circunstancia,* "I am myself and my circumstance." To apply it to writers in particular one might add: "as I am trying to conquer time and space through writing." The formula could be extended to a literary generation.

A difficult choice has to be made since it is neither possible nor desirable to mention the hundred or more artists and writers belonging chronologically to the Independence Generation. It would also be unfair to exclude any who did not adhere to the *Pró-Cultura* movement, particularly writers who chose to live abroad, e.g., in the United States, and for reasons of their own disregarded appeals to assist in the building of a new society at home.

Apart from two older writers, Arménio Vieira and Corsino Fortes, who must be considered because of their lasting impact, seven individuals born between 1950 and 1965 have come to represent the Generation in my opinion. I have chosen them because of their craftsmanship, their aesthetic appeal and the depth of their work, achieved through personal experience.

Two Models

Two elders, men now in their forties, have had a dominant influence on recent Cape Verdean literature, and on poetry in particular, thanks to their position, their personality, and the novelty of their literary style within the Cape Verdean context.

ARMÉNIO VIEIRA has the more striking personality of the two. He knows a great deal of literature, is a witty, sharp-tongued conversationalist and has created for himself the paradoxical aura of a publicly visible loner. He is said to go and play chess on weekends at a scenic spot, the *Prainha* ("Little Beach") outside the town. During the week he can be found in the center of town, at the *Vulcão* ("Volcano"), a tiny, dark café on the *Plateau*, writing as he is sitting by himself at one of its tables. The *Vulcão* is near the offices of *Voz di Povo*, where he earns his bread and butter as a journalist. He thus stands out as an individualist in a society that discourages individuality. Once he has been engaged in a conversation he begins to tell stories, revealing an exuberant, mordant and at the same time sociable temperament, as if inspired by the explosive force that usually lies dormant within the mighty *Fogo* volcano depicted on the mural behind him. When asked about a book published recently in the new Creole spelling with its many "k"s and "ĉ"s and "ĵ"s, he said that the author had made sure no reader would understand his profound message. When I talked to him, Vieira did not say anything about himself or his own work until asked what interested him. Then he merely replied that he was interested in observing the way in which people around him were behaving.

Vieira is a native of Praia, where he was born in 1941. However, like many intellectually gifted young people in earlier times, he went to school at the *liceu* in Mindelo on São Vicente Island before doing his military service in Portugal. Upon his return he worked as a meteorologist and journalist. In the early 1960s his poems began to appear in literary supplements and journals. He had to wait until 1981 for the publication of a collection of later poetry in Portugal, *Poemas 1971–1979*, which in a way made him a contemporary of the Independence Generation. These poems of his mature years reflect a variety of moods. Some are *lenga-lengas*, mere literary games played with letters or words. Others are irreverent, satirical or sarcastic pieces, but written always in defense of a noble cause, human dignity. Such are the early poems *Isto é o que fazem de nós* ("This Is What They Do to Us") and *Toti Cadabra*, which echoes the Brazilian Cabral de Melo Neto's most incisive poem on the hopelessly poor in the harsh interior of northeastern Brazil, *Morte e Vida Severina* ("Death and Life of People like Severino.")

Vieira possesses a great facility to adopt the style of other poets when he wants to, e.g., the prophetic and epic manner of João Varela or the symbolic inventions of Corsino Fortes. In general, as in his love poems, the undertone is dead serious. He appears to be haunted by the transitoriness of life, fame, memory, affection. Once upon a time, before 1974, he had raised his voice in the chorus of patriotic protesters of the *Sèló* supplement when that was important. He also had written ringing verse in Creole during the months preceding Independence, even a national anthem, *Nôs bandera* ("Our Flag"). But afterwards he broadened his outlook, seeing a future Cape Verde as participating in a fuller life for all of humankind, a more humane civilization. Well versed in western mythology and literature, he mastered a variety of rhythms and themes, verse forms and images. Aside from poetry, he has written *crónicas* (prose sketches) and brief, quirky ghost stories, for example one in which a ghost nearly kills a person out of kindness.

Vieira's venture into "new spaces," beyond Cape Verdean insularity, was hailed by one of the *Pró-Cultura* writers, José Vicente Lopes, in the essay *Novas estruturas poéticas e temáticas da poesia caboverdiana* ("New Poetic and Thematic Structures of Cape Verdean Poetry"), which *Ponto & Vírgula* published (no. 16, pp. 19–23.) He, too, found it refreshing that

Vieira was dealing with the "broader reality" of the human condition, using the ancient myths of Sisyphus, Venus and Apollo in a modern, sarcastic way to express his preoccupation about the future.

The other elder brother of the Independence Generation, CORSINO FORTES, was born in the city of Mindelo in 1933. Trained as a lawyer in Lisbon, he was sent to Angola as a judge in 1957. Since 1975, the year of Cape Verdean independence, he has served his nation as a diplomat.

Fortes's earliest poems, such as *Mindelo* and *Meio-Dia* ("Noon"), appeared in 1959/60, but the first volumes of a trilogy, his most ambitious undertaking so far, were published only in 1974 as *Pão & fonema* ("Bread and Phoneme") and in 1986 as *Árvore & tambor* ("Tree and Drum") respectively. Thus, like Arménio Vieira's book, they were bound to mold the poets of the Independence Generation. Fortes is preparing *Sol & substância* ("Sun and Substance"), the final volume.

The haunting language of his hermetic poetry no doubt raised a barrier between him and many of the educated Cape Verdeans, not to mention the mass of his people. But it challenged the younger writers. Some, like Arménio Vieira at times and José Vicente Lopes consistently, would imitate it, while scholars, such as the Cape Verdean ethnographer Mesquitela Lima and the literary specialists Pires Laranjeira and Ana Mafalda Leite in Portugal attempted learned explications of Fortes's intentions. Of course, like any writer, he wants very much to be understood. In 1986, during a conversation at the *Claridade* Symposium, he made it clear that he was not merely playing with language, as his delight in alliterations and seemingly arbitrary juxtapositions might indicate, but that he had meditated the form of his trilogy for years before its publication so that new ways of using the language would correspond to the reshaping of Cape Verdean society. His rhythms possess the monotony of mighty hammer blows. Instead of charming with word music, he invites his readers' collaboration to discover new meanings he was giving to words.

Another interpretation is possible, as was pointed out by R. Hamilton (*Literatura africana-literatura necessária*, vol. II, p. 207): Fortes may have written *Pão & fonema* with the idea of halting the Cape Verdean urge to emigrate, an "escapist" urge other poets had symbolized as a utopia, the dreamland of Pasárgada, taking their cue from the Brazilian poet Manuel Bandeira. Fortes expressed the anti-evasion sentiment vehemently in the form of an appeal to his former schoolmate from Mindelo, João Varela, which figures prominently in *Pão & fonema*. In the seventies, however, *anti-evasionismo* was no longer a new theme.

Still another reading would concentrate on the style of the work. Since it was conceived before 1974 and parts of it had been published in Lisbon when the literary censorship of Salazar's and Caetano's *Estado Novo* regime discouraged political anti-imperialism, the author had adopted a labyrinthine style to hide his revolutionary desire for Cape Verdean independence behind apparently meaningless conglomerates of words. For example, one discovers in the poem *Emigrante* that the objective lines

Cresce
Um progresso de pedra morta
("There grows/a progress of dead stone")

are followed by the provocative

Que a Península
              Ainda bebe
Pela taça da colónia
Todo o sangue do teu corpo peregrino

(For the [Iberian] Peninsula
              still drinks
in its colonial cup
all the blood of your peregrine body" [p. 39])

or in the poem *De rosto a sotavento* ("Facing Leeward"), the initial surrealism of

Há mãos que cantam
              No rosto da página
("Hands there are that sing/On the face of the page")

ends a page later with the shout

              Não consintam
Que o tempo roube à minha fome
O ovo do sol que nasce. . .

              (Do not consent
that time should snatch from my hunger
the egg of the sun to be born . . ." [p. 60])

Could one not conclude that such a style, adopted out of necessity, became an experimental novelty inviting other poets to adopt it? It was refreshingly different from the tested models offered by the *Claridade* writers.

Back to Universals

Because of his spirit of initiative, José Luís Hopffer C. Almada deserves first place as a leading figure in *Pró-Cultura*, the only movement of the Generation. Born about 1965 in the small market town of Santa Catarina on Santiago Island, José Luís spent many years in East Germany as a university student. His poetry has to be searched for in periodicals, where it appeared from 1986 on, not under his own name but under the pen names "Zé di Sant'y Agu," "Alma Dofer" and "Erasmo Cabral d'Almada." A many-sided author, he adopted "Tuna Furtado" to sign prose, such as editorials, and "Dionísio de Deus y Fonteana" as the author of stories, but used his given name when delving into literary history, as in an article paying homage to the memory of Baltazar Lopes or for introductions to writings of other dead authors. In 1986 he became the shaker and mover of *Pró-Cultura* and the editor of its review *Frag-*

mentos. His published poems add up to about a dozen. Like his programmatical editorials, they reveal his hesitation among several possible paths to be taken, as if he were still uncertain of his identity. In *Buska* ("The Search"), one of his Creole poems, he wrote in 1988 that he needed to find out what the world was really like in order to find *nha kabesa,* "my own head." His poems on Cape Verdean themes sadly seem to question the success of efforts that were being made to change the Islands—*verde afã ou uma palavra vã?* ("Green endeavor or any empty word?") Other poems turn on general human concerns, the pains of love (*Angústia,* "Anguish," 1986) and death (*A eternidade veio,* "Eternity Arrived," 1987). Contemplation of suicide appears in a prose piece about madness (*Março,* "The Month of March," 1987). Once he has found his way, perhaps through a synthesis of the several tendencies that beckon to him, he may well produce a poetry of deeper insights.

"Binga," whose official name is ALBERTO FERREIRA GOMES, came into the world in 1957 in the port city of Mindelo. He emigrated to Portugal in 1977 but returned a year later and became a meteorologist on Sal Island, where he has been living ever since. For professional training he also spent some time in Angola about 1979, and it was there that he composed his earliest known poetry. By now he has published many poems and stories. Much of his writing is dominated by the general human wish to escape from a depressing reality into a fantasy world. He steers clear of ideology and politics. One of his earliest poems, *Tamarindeiro mártir* ("The Martyred Tamarind") combines a touch of ecological thought with nostalgic childhood memories. He wrote it in Angola and it was first published in the Catholic review *Terra Nova* of February 1980. In another poem he exalted the serenaders of the Islands as *Peregrins d'paz* ("Pilgrims of Peace," 1987). A third, *Insaciável* ("Insatiable," 1985) portrayed the goddess of Poetry as an insatiable female, dwelling in an "unreal realm devoid of carnal contact."

Close to the Rural Folk

Several fascinating authors were born in or about 1950. The most versatile and perhaps most productive of them is TOMÉ VARELA DA SILVA, a steadfast champion of the Cape Verdean Creole language. He has published two volumes of poetry, *Kumuñon d'Áfrika: Onti, osî, mañan* ("Communion with Africa: Yesterday, Today, Tomorrow," 1986) and *Kardisantus* ("Thistles," 1987), a collection of stories, *Natal y kontus* ("Christmas and Stories," 1988), and he has edited and commented on folk singers of his native island in *Finasons di ña Nasia Gomi* ("Tune-up Songs of Mrs. Anastasia Gomes," 1985) and *Ña Bibiña Kabral, bida-óbra* ("Mrs. Mimi Cabral, Her Life and Work," 1988), the latter in collaboration with Alexandre Semedo. He also enlisted Semedo's help to gather and edit the island's living folktales, calling the collection *Na bóka noti,* vol. I ("At Nightfall,"

1987), noteworthy as the first scholarly collection produced by Cape Verdeans and within Cape Verde.

T.V. da Silva was born in 1950 at São Jorge dos Órgãos, a village in the rugged mountains of Santiago Island. He was trained as a farm agent at its agricultural school but went to Portugal to study theology in Braga, then gave up the idea of becoming a priest and worked as a miner for three years. In 1981 he returned to his homeland and was placed in charge of the Department of Oral Traditions, a section of the Ministry of Education and Culture in Praia.

He is the only writer of his generation daring to write almost exclusively in Creole, even introductions, explanations of phonetics, and descriptions of his methods as a folklorist. With some exaggeration, his friend Oswaldo Osório remarked in one preface, "Today we find an almost unanimous tendency among young poets to use Creole" (in the preface to Carlos Barbosa's, *Vinti ŝintidu letradu na kriolu*, 1984). In T.V.'s case, the tendency is a natural one, springing from his roots in rural Santiago, where African traditions are more alive than anywhere else in Cape Verde. Thus, he wrote only five of the fifty poems making up *Kumuñon d'Áfrika* in standard Portuguese between 1971 and 1982, years spent in Portugal for the most part.

His poems sound and feel genuine. They speak not only of "his own doubts and hopes concerning the future, of his Mother, his Land, (. . .) always inspired by great love, an act of moral and political courage" (Osório in the preface to *Kumuñon*). One of the four sections of the book bears the title *Inketason*, "Worry," while the last is called *Intervenson*, "Doing Something About It." But he also voices the perplexities of the ordinary people. Ending his own introduction on a humorous note, he wished that his poems would be "a pinch of snuff in the nose of conscience," or else "a spoonful of honesty in the cup of thought as it is raised to the mouth of feeling." The dedication of the volume "to all human humanists in every place, time and culture" shows that it was not only intended for African readers. Whenever T.V. uses Creole, his language is musical, strongly rhythmical, and usually concentrated in short stanzas or poems resembling folk sayings and songs.

Likewise, though dealing with real situations in the hard lives of the islanders, his stories end happily, like folktales, perhaps also because of the traditional faith that is part of his Christian upbringing. But just as in the works of most writers in this generation, mentions of specific people or of his family are strikingly absent, in contrast to the practice of preceding generations.

The rapidly written Christmas stories testify to his inventive use of a literary genre that was new to him. They are of uneven quality. One of the more original and successful ones is *Natal*, "Christmas," in which the Christ Child becomes a Cape Verdean youngster.

ALEXANDRE (SANCHES) SEMEDO, who adopted the pen name "Alsasem," hails from the interior of Santiago, like T.V. da Silva. He was born in 1956.

Also like Silva, he knows how to appreciate the folklore of his region. He belonged to the leadership of the official youth organization and co-edited *Seiva*, its monthly magazine, in Praia before joining the Office for Cooperatives recently. He has taught in a trade school.

Only a few of his literary writings have been published so far: some newspaper feature articles, mostly about folklore, and several poems. Among his manuscripts he is holding back numerous poems that fore-shadow the makings of an original author. His ambition has not yet gone beyond the important one of serving as a good youth leader, as is apparent from his plea for youth, *Pessimismo e anseio* ("Pessimism and Yearning"). He also aims to be an honest reporter who, unlike some others, refuses to hide the true state of affairs from the reader, as he made clear in the article *Não aceitarei bluff* ("I Shall not Accept Bluff," 1986).

The Cape Verdeans he admires most are the writers A. A. Gonçalves and Arménio Vieira, because of their stories, and the irrepressible folk singer Mimi Cabral. His poems manifest considerable versatility. His pref-erence goes to short, sententious ones that are almost epigrams. He also has tried his hand at concrete poetry. While he wants very much to be a useful citizen (see for example his poem *Querença*, "Desire," 1987), he has moments when the fatalism so widespread among his people over-whelms him also, so that he is driven to write poems such as *Banalidade* (1987) and the seven-liner *E então* ("And so," 1988), which ends:

> . . . da minha raça / (. . .) / sentenciada pelo fardo da desgraça.

> (". . . of my race / . . . / crushed below the weight of doom.")

Another epigram of his, *Jornalista* (1987), asked journalists to show courage but ended with a combined question/exclamation mark. At other times, he could write lighthearted verse. His earliest verses known to me were published in *Terra Nova* in 1981.

Formal Experimentation

JORGE CARLOS FONSECA has published poetry since at least 1976. He was born in Mindelo in 1950. In 1972, his final year as a student at the University of Coimbra, Portugal, he was expelled for having engaged in political activity that was offensive to the Portuguese dictator. Eventually that was to help him gain a position in the Ministry of Foreign Affairs of his native land when Cape Verde became independent. However, he left the Islands in 1979 to live in Lisbon. In 1979 he paid a visit to New York City and wrote at least two poems about that experience.

Poems by Fonseca are found in *Jogos florais 1976* ("Floral Games 1976"), an anthology, and also now and then in periodicals. Originating in day-dreams, they are strung together in a slightly surrealistic manner. They sing of beauty, abundance, happiness, and the "sowing of tomorrow's Revolution" (with a capital R). Disillusionment lurks in the background and must be warded off, e.g., in *Poema do destemor* ("Poem of Fearless-ness," *Jogos florais*), where "a shipwreck is threatening." The dithyrambic rhythms, which are characteristic of him, seem inspired by dances. The word "revolution" appears rarely, whereas "death," "excrement," "disguise" and "liberty" recur frequently.

All of Fonseca's poems that I have seen date from 1978 or before and one wonders if inspiration has abandoned him since then. He continues, however, to publish them. In its nos. 5/6 (November 1989), *Fragmentos* included one disillusioned poem written while he was in Praia in the summer of 1978. It consists of four unanswered questions couched in free verse and exhibiting irrational combinations of nouns and adjectives like his other poems: "playful ashtray," "plasticized soirées of smiling days," "orange-colored paralysis." The poet ends this poem by wondering why silence has driven out poetry:

> E porque esta insónia negra
> de vermelhas querer ver
> as madrugadas todas
> de nossos poemas soletrados e banidos pelo silêncio?

> (And why this black insomnia
> of wanting to see reddening
> every dawn
> of our poems, poems now spelled and banished by silence?)

JORGE TOLENTINO, also writing under the pseudonym "Moninfeudo," is the youngest of the seven. Born in Mindelo in 1963, he also studied in Portugal. Like Hopffer Almada and Semedo, he promises to develop into a major writer.

Different from the others, he has preferred thus far to write prose rather than poetry. Three stories of his have appeared since 1980, each in a different periodical. In a fourth periodical, *Fragmentos*, no. 1, 1987, he published the first act of a verse drama, as an experiment in that art form, the least cultivated in Cape Verde. Tolentino's little drama bears no title. Using the hackneyed comic situation of a drunk's arrest and interrogation, he gives the scene a depressing racial meaning. In the dark street no passer-by had come to the drunken black man's rescue. He and two other prisoners find themselves accused of heinous deeds which they have not committed. The scene is set in what seems to be a Portuguese city. The drunk is a Cape Verdean. There is no visual ending. Instead, a Creole poem, Corsino Fortes' *Ó konde palmanhã manchê* ("Oh, when the Dawn Arrived") is recited as an expression of the messianic hope of the wretched of this earth.

Among Tolentino's stories, *Brisas de ontem* ("Breezes of Yesteryear") is the longest and best. Actually it grew into a novella. Written in 1979, it did not appear until 1984 in the review *Raízes*. In a matter-of-fact way, its prose, as A. A. Gonçalves's had done so successfully, reproduced the tense atmosphere of the life of the poor in the Cape Verdean towns. The language suggested Creole through sparing but telling use of certain Island idioms. The story was told from a boy's perspective, who observes his parents' struggle for survival, the father being one of the thousands of islanders unable to find sufficient employment and therefore deciding to leave and seek his fortune abroad, while the mother stays behind to take care of four children as best she can. It is a wonderful tale, faithful to reality, in praise of women's courage and resourcefulness. The night breeze that blows through the story seems to promise a better dawn at some future day. It is not the way the story unfolds that is so striking as the economy of means with which it is told. In that respect it represents a reaction against the elaborate, somewhat florid prose that has dominated Portuguese literature in the wake of Eça de Queiroz's masterworks.

Expatriates

ADELINA C. DA SILVA, a Fogo Islander, born in 1958, went to school in Praia, emigrated to the United States when she was eighteen, about which time she began to write poetry. She now lives and teaches in Roxbury, Massachusetts. From 1985 on, her poems have been published in Teobaldo Virgínio de Melo's review *Arquipélago*, a purely Cape Verdean publication issued in Boston.

At first glance, it appears strange that the Independence Generation includes so few women, in contrast to the large number of prominent feminine writers in contemporary Brazil and Portugal. Only three come to mind: Adelina da Silva, Vera Duarte (born in Mindelo, 1952), "Lara Araújo" (born on Sal in 1951). Upon reflection, one may surmise that one cause might well be that schooling was reserved for boys until very recently.

Passionate, though more restrained than the less frustrated and frankly sensual Vera Duarte, Silva celebrates the universal need for love as women feel it. Her verses flow melodiously in waves of rhythmic motion. She is, however, capable of forceful appeals, as in *Irmão* ("Brother," in *Arquipélago*, no. 3, February 1986):

>   Escuta irmão
>   meu grito é forte d'arma nova
>   que quer penetrar teu sangue
>   tua alma
>   Escuta irmão
>   [. . .]
>   Vem viver comigo nossa vida crioula
>   e vê se vale a pena ou não
>   o meu apelo, minha poesia caboverdeana.

>   ("Listen brother
>   my cry is sharp, a new sword
>   ready to pierce your blood
>   your soul
>   Listen brother
>   [. . .]
>   Come share with me our Creole life
>   and see if there is value or not
>   in my verse, my call for Cape Verde.")

The pages of the journals *Fragmentos, Ponto & Vírgula, Magma, Seiva, Voz di Letra, Tribuna,* etc., contain stories, prose sketches, poems by dozens of other authors mostly belonging to the same Independence Generation as the ones mentioned, such as Jó Spínola, José Luís Hopffer C. Almada's closest collaborator, Mark Dennis Velhinho Rodrigues, "Nicolau de Topo Vermelho" (José Maria Ramos), "Sukre d'Sal" (Francisco Tomar) or the essayist José Vicente Lopes. The editors of those journals have enjoyed the strong support of older and well known writers, foremost among them Corsino Fortes, Arménio Vieira, Oliveira Barros, and Oswaldo Osório.

CONCLUSIONS:
FREEDOM, DIVERSITY AND HUMANISM

On the basis of the biographies and the available writings of the members of the Independence Generation of the Cape Verde Islands several generalizations can be made. They relate to external circumstances, not to the intrinsic character of the literature.

It is the first generation which found its focus in Praia, the national capital, and not in Mindelo, known as *Porto Grande* for really having been the "Great Port" city of the Islands. Of sixteen writers born since 1950, seven live in Praia, only one in Mindelo, four on Sal Island, and four live abroad. It is also significant that more than half of the sixty-odd poets represented in J.L. Hopffer C. Almada's projected *Mirabilis* anthology received their advanced education at the Liceu Domingos Ramos in Praia. In contrast, of the fifteen writers born between 1900 and 1925 who were included in Baltasar Lopes's *Antologia da ficção cabo-verdiana contemporânea* (1960) and Manuel Ferreira's anthology of poetry *No reino de Caliban*, vol. I (1975), eight went to the Liceu in Mindelo, although only four were born there and of these, one, Sérgio Frusoni, received his schooling elsewhere. None attended a *liceu* in Praia.

The Independence Generation did not rebel against its elders, as prominent members of the preceding generation had done when they attacked *Claridade*, accusing that group of escapism in the name of social revolution, Africanization and the elevation of *Caboverdiano*, their name for Cape Verdean Creole, to the role as *the* national and literary language.

In the third place, this Generation continued to use standard Portuguese for most of its writings, with the exception of two or three writers, notably T.V. da Silva.

Turning to internal features, what characterizes the spirit of the Independence Generation? What is new in its thought and in its creations? Does it follow a specific literary program? Many in the Generation, perhaps all by now, reject what they term "pamphlet" art and literature, that is, what the present, aging political leadership prescribed as constructive, because it would contribute to the rapid, conscious formation of the classless "new society." According to that thought, socially "progressive" intentions and goals were to be emphasized, without any regard to beauty of expression. No doubt, the leaders of the revolutionary regime assumed that the fervor which had inspired anti-colonial writing would last and be transferred to a social program along the Marxist-Leninist model. Instead, the revolutionary bards ran out of breath: "Kwame Kondé" (Francisco Fragoso), Gabriel Mariano, Ovídio Martins, Onésimo Silveira, Emanuel Braga Tavares. Stated positively, the new Generation

23

insisted on artistic freedom for itself, leaving it up to the individual artist
or writer what and how he wanted to create. Aesthetic quality has again
been placed above orthodoxy. At least since the nineteen eighties a less
utopian, more realistic view of Cape Verdean development, accompanied by disillusion, has led to liberalization. Interestingly, the review
Seiva mentioned the *perestroika* reconstruction of Soviet Russian life. A picture of Soviet president Gorbachev illustrated a sampling of the opinions
of five young Cape Verdeans. When asked which foreign politicians they
considered outstanding, three of them named Gorbachev, two Nelson
Mandela, one Arafat (*Seiva*, no. 8, January 1989.)

The relative liberalization owed something to the moderating
influence of respected writers, most of whom had been members of the
Claridade group, devoted to the Islands, even though choosing to live
abroad, such as Manuel Lopes, Teixeira de Sousa, Orlanda Amarilis and
Yolanda Morazzo. Actual resistance to orthodox Marxism came from the
Catholic opposition gathered around the journal *Terra Nova*, edited by
Friar António Fidalgo Barros, who used to write patriotic poetry. Barros
had engaged an expatriate living in Brazil, the writer Luís Romano, to
direct the literary section of the journal. Both helped to preserve standard Portuguese as the principal literary language, without disdaining
Creole.

A similar change, a return to literature as art, has been taking place
elsewhere. In Angola, "the young poets put aside poetry as a weapon
in the 1970s. [One of them,] David Mestre defined the project of renewal:
We wanted and still want to give equal weight to ethics and aesthetics."
Thus was the change summed up by a Brazilian anthologist, Cremilde
de A. Medina in *Sonha mamana África* ("Dream, Dear Mother Africa," São
Paulo, 1987, p. 363). In Mozambique a prominent poet, Luís Carlos Patra-
quim, wrote for publication in *JL, Jornal de Letras, Artes e Ideias* (Lisbon,
no. 347, February 28, 1989): "In the generation coming to the fore since
Independence (. . .) the greatest diversity possible is now beginning to
take shape." And of another young Mozambican poet, Heliodoro Bap-
tista, he remarked: "He is one of the most serious poets, with a critical
mind and an original discourse, who keeps his distance from what had
been the militant rhetoric attuned to official optimism about the
country's historic evolution."

As in Angola, Mozambique and the other former colonies of Portugal,
the linguistic battle has for the foreseeable future been decided in favor
of standard Portuguese. In none are the "national" African languages
even taught in the elementary schools. At the same time, in Cape Verde,
as in those other countries, writing is slowly gaining ground in what
had been only spoken languages until the dawn of the twentieth century,
and so has awareness of the oral traditions on the part of the urban
intellectuals.

Another position of the Independence Generation is the search for
what is universally human in the Cape Verdean experience. "T.T. Tiofe"
(João Varela) diagnosed the trend in *Arte poética e artefactos poéticos em Cabo*

Verde ("Poetic Art and Poetic Artefacts in Cape Verde"), a paper he read in Paris in November 1984: "As has happened in other countries, some time after their access to sovereignty, poetry no longer limits itself to the interpretation of circumstantial, local geopolitical data. It is beginning to meditate on the people of the Archipelago as links in the chain of onto-logical vicissitudes that are universal to man" (*Les littératures africaines de langue portugaise*, Paris, 1985, p. 315).

Art, freedom, diversity and humanism are the ideals that the Genera-tion is attempting to carry out.

As to the achievements, the verdict is not yet in. The Independence Generation has not yet completed its productive stage. So far the achieve-ments are modest, as was stated by José Luís Hopffer C. Almada himself: "To tell the truth, mediocrity is rampant in our towns. Sometimes I have the impression of living in the Wonderland where a one-eyed man is king of the blind" (*Seiva*, no. 8, January 1989, p. 14). Some good poetry has been produced, but most verse seems rather formless and unpoetic. Prose writing is gaining ground. Like the poems, the prose narratives usually are short. But recently, two authors belonging to the Generation published first full-length novels; so far no full-fledged play or extended poem has been produced.

It has taken two not much older writers to fill the void to a degree, and thus set examples. In 1987, Manuel Veiga, who was born in 1948, pub-lished *Oju d'Águ* ("Wellspring"), an allegorical novel wholly composed in Cape Verdean Creole. And in 1990, Arménio Vieira's symbolical novel *O eleito do sol* ("The Sun's Chosen") appeared. As for plays, a comedy showed one way to create a viable theater. Based on folk entertainment, it was written by a popular composer-poet known as "Ano Novo," Sá de Bonjardim. He combined poetry, song and dance. For the actors who played the parts of authorities the speeches were written in standard Portuguese, for those playing commoners, in Creole. Hopffer Almada printed the comedy in nos. 5/6 (November 1989) of *Fragmentos*.

An incomplete spectrum of literary production, like the one seen so far among the Independence Generation, is not peculiar to Cape Verde. In Angola, which also can draw on a large pool of young writers, most good literature continues to flow from the pens of writers who had proven their worth before Independence.

It is not merely a question of the dearth of economic resources that makes publication a rare privilege in Cape Verde. A decisive delaying factor proves to be the necessity for the nation of recent independence to engage its relatively few trained communicators, such as highly edu-cated writers, in administrative tasks that consume time and energy, aside from imposing a limit to any public expression of criticism.

When the nations of the New World became independent it took at least fifty years until writers appeared whose works could measure up to and surpass the earlier generations that had prepared national inde-pendence. Only then did a national literature begin to take shape that could gain worldwide attention. When Brazil was given its independence without a struggle in 1822, it already had produced a generation of good poets, several of whom (for example, Cláudio da Costa) were involved in a political conspiracy against the Portuguese crown. It took until 1871 for a greater poet, Castro Alves, to publish his *Espumas flutuantes* ("Floating Foam"), followed by a literary man of genius, Machado de Assis, becoming famous from 1872 on, the year when he published his first collection of tales, the *Contos fluminenses* ("Carioca Tales").

When the United States gained its independence after 1776 by force of arms, it could claim several authors of good prose, though none of good poetry: Paine, Franklin, Jefferson. The first works that continue to rank high in American literature appeared only from the 1830s on: Poe's *Poems* in 1831, *Nature*, Emerson's first essay, in 1836, and Hawthorne's novel *The Scarlet Letter* in 1850. What the British critic Marcus Cunliffe said of American literature, that "political independence did not bring cultural independence" immediately, seems to apply generally (*The Literature of the United States*, Harmondsworth, 1954, p. 42).

Does literary evolution proceed at a faster pace now? I find it more likely that at least one more generation or two will be needed on the Cape Verde Islands for artists and writers to furnish the utmost creative effort, fulfilling Emerson's prophecy that "events, actions arise that must be sung." What else he said, about "the literature of the poor being the topic of the time" again became true in the Cape Verdean case, but has little to do with artistic quality. Even the relatively modest achievements of the Independence Generation to date deserve admiration, like the works of its predecessors; for they represent triumphs over many handicaps— climate, shortages of all kinds, ideological constraints—a struggle that has to be waged over and over again. How many small countries can point to such an array of earnest young intellectuals, striving to take their place in a literature and a language whose roots reach back to ancient Rome and Athens? With a population basis of only about 325,000 in the mid-nineteen sixties and a capital of 39,000 souls in 1980, the Islands' literature compares favorably with that of the 573,000 people of neighboring Guinea-Bissau on the continent, with the European nations of Luxembourg, Iceland and Malta, or with the islands of Martinique and Guadeloupe in the Americas. To be sure, Cape Verde has one advantage: its people roam the earth. Those who, like the *Merkone* ("Americans"), return, bringing back new ideas, skills, experiences, possessions and *encomendas* (goods requested by their relatives), all of which, taken together, stimulate through contact with richer and more developed countries—Portugal, Italy, France, the Netherlands, Norway, Germany, the United States, and Venezuela. However, there may be a fly in the ointment: the power of routine. Take the case of a young Cape Verdean from a farming family on Santiago Island, who went to study business management in Tucson, Arizona, thanks to a scholarship. Upon his return he became director of a state-subsidized bus company. In an interview he declared to *Seiva* (no. 1, November 1986):

I returned in 1984 and what I found did not come up to my expectations. As is normal, I brought back new ideas, dynamism, the will to work hard and to experiment. But I ran into barriers and restrictions, and that's where my frustration began. I believe the problem is common for the vast majority of young people who have just finished their studies. No one has confidence in them.

What I learned about the thought and writings of the Cape Verdean generation that was molded by national Independence contradicted some earlier assumptions and confirmed others. It is true that the literary tendencies of young Cape Verdean writers are similar to those of other lusophone writers in Africa, for example, their rejection of purely "militant" literature. I also found that resignation no longer characterizes Cape Verdean writing, in spite of the unchanging physical environment. Creole has not made as much progress as I had expected. Africanization apparently has been placed in abeyance. Mindelo no longer dominates culturally, having been replaced by Praia, although it retains some importance, especially in music, the arts, crafts and printing.

I did meet a specific "Independence Generation," but it was not so coherent and homogeneous as I had imagined. Its writers were producing and publishing more than I believed possible. Some of their writings hold the promise that the Generation may truly become *Mirabilis*.

POSTSCRIPT I: SHORT-LIVED OR DORMANT?

What has happened to the *Pró-Cultura* movement during the two years since the spring of 1990? Its story can be told briefly, all too briefly. It came to an unexpected, untimely halt. Could its impetus not be sustained? Will it revive? That is the question.

The stagnation of *Pró-Cultura* may be due to a variety of causes. One reason could be its origin as the brainchild of one young man, whose frequent and prolonged absences from the Islands diminished his effectiveness as a leader.

Another reason would be lack of funding. How could the group afford the cost of its organ, *Fragmentos*, and of other ambitious projects, such as *Mirabilis*, an anthology intended to include *hundreds* of poems?[1] (The latter has still not materialized and *Fragmentos* had to cease publication after merely four, though very large, issues.) One ought to remember that a very small number of the Islanders are readers of poetry or prose fiction, not enough to sustain a purely literary publication, even if one adds the many emigrants and their descendants in countries such as Portugal, the United States, Canada, the Netherlands, etc. Books seem to have found readers more readily, at least until recently, before their price rose steeply.

A third, weighty reason for stagnation, if not demise, could be political: the collapse suffered by the monolithic Leninist-Marxist regime of the PAICV (Partido Africano pela Independência de Cabo Verde) when free elections led to its replacement by a moderate, procapitalistic government in early 1991. The *Pró-Cultura* movement had foreshadowed the change by its insistence on pluralism and on freedom from ideological constraints. Immediately, the material support ceased which the previous regime gave at least indirectly to cultural institutions, such as the *Instituto Caboverdiano do Livro e do Disco*, the publisher and distributor of literature. Artists and writers—in short, cultural life—could not count on further subsidies during this transitional period.

Uncertainty did not mean that the Generation ceased its activity, however. To be sure José Luís Hopffer Almada's promising movement shows no sign of life yet, as far as I can see,[2] in spite of his protestations to the contrary, when he assured me that "our *Pró-Cultura–Fragmentos* move-

---

[1] Referring to *Mirabilis*, A. Semedo remarked in a letter of May 21, 1990: "The cost of it is rather steep—around almost 1.000.000 Cape Verdean escudos [over US $15,000], while patronage is still a rarity."

[2] "J.L. Hopffer Almada has by now returned to Cape Verde, but *Pró-Cultura* seems to be forgotten, according to my informants." Quoted from a letter of November 4, 1991, by a correspondent living in Mindelo.

ment continues and perseveres," . . . "the seventh issue of *Fragmentos* is already with the printer," . . . and "the *Mirabilis—De Veias ao sol* anthology will see the light of day before the year ends."[3]

While Hopffer Almada's hopes remain unfulfilled, new writings by his generation continue to appear. Daniel Spínola, also publishing under the pen name "Euricles Rodrigues," issued *Lágrimas de bronze* ("Bronze Tears"), a booklet of short stories (Praia, 1990) and *Na cantar di sol* ("In the Canto of the Sun"), a collection of poems in Creole (Praia, 1991). He had been the co-editor of *Fragmentos*. T.V. da Silva's folklore essay introducing a volume of stories told by Guida Mendes, a woman of the people, appeared in 1990, the year after Vasco Martins, the poet and musicologist had published an essay, *Morna*, about the folk dance and song by that name. Moreover, Martins and a second writer attempted the first extended prose fiction to be written by members of the generation, Vasco Martins's novel *A verdadeira dimensão* ("The True Dimension," Linda-A-Velha, Portugal, 1990) and Carlos Araújo's *Percurso vulgar*, also a novel ("An Ordinary Course of Events," Mindelo, 1990). Araújo was born in Paúl on Santo Antão Island, 1950. What is as significant, a new journal sought to fill the void left by *Fragmentos* and *Seiva*, the two periodicals closest to *Pró-Cultura*. It bears the name *Artiletra*. Proclaiming its mission to be a journal of *intercâmbio cultural* (cultural interchange), it began publication in May 1991. It also signaled a shift from Praia, the capital of the Islands, back to Mindelo on São Vicente Island, once their commercial and cultural center, where the periodical *Claridade* had inaugurated the rise of Cape Verdean consciousness in the 1930s, half a century ago.

POSTSCRIPT II: UPBEAT ONE YEAR LATER

In June 1992, a new issue, no. 7/8, of *Fragmentos*, arrived in Pennsylvania, with the date of December 1991. It provided confirmation of what I had learned a couple of months earlier: the anthology *Mirabilis—De Veias ao sol* had likewise been published at the very end of 1991, but by a Portuguese publisher (with the subtitle *Antologia dos novíssimos poetas caboverdianos*. Lisbon, Ed. Caminho, 1991. 523 pages.)

In a "Notice," the editorial board, including J. L. Hopffer Almada, let it be known that "We shall continue as before to be a critical voice inherent in the communion between ethics and aesthetics" and that "other issues will shortly appear." (*Fragmentos*, no. 7/8, p. 2.) Referring to the political changeover, they hailed it: "The profound changes through which the country has gone merely prove those right who have always

---

[3] J.L. Hopffer Almada, in a letter of March 22, 1990.

fought for pluralism and the useful co-existence of diverse tendencies, as in the case of us promoters of the review *Fragmentos*" (ibid). The political upheaval delayed both publications, which had been ready since the end of 1989. They give tangible proof of continuity.

In the same issue J. L. Hopffer Almada's editorial and his lengthy, well-informed and balanced essay "A poesia caboverdiana e os caminhos da nova geração" (Cape Verdean Poetry and the Roads Taken by the New Generation)[4] show his pride in what has been accomplished so far and of more to be expected from *Pró-Cultura* and the generation it represents. In the editorial he lists the most prominent among the "countless activities" of *Pró-Cultura* since its beginnings in March 1986:

> Our part in conceiving and bringing about *Voz di Letra* [the literary supplement of the journal *Voz di Povo* in Praia, co-edited by O. Osório and Ondina Ferreira];
>
> The weekly radio program "People, Ideas, Culture" during one whole year;
>
> The first Week of Integrated Art, including the largest exhibition of plastic and graphic arts held to date in Praia;
>
> Publication of the review *Fragmentos*;
>
> Talks, poetry and music recitals, in a word, stirring up the cultural routine;
>
> Support for the publication of books by young authors; and
>
> The anthology of poetry *Mirabilis—De veias ao sol* ("Veins in the Sun").
>
> (ibid, 9)

In "A novíssima geração de poetas," a section of the essay, José Luís coins the term *fragmentarismo*, giving it a symbolic meaning: "*Fragmentarismo*, as a form of co-existence of poetic contemporaneity, signifies aesthetic pluralism and the plurality of being Cape Verdean" (ibid, 17). He considers this fragmentary tendency to be the essential feature of the review *Fragmentos*, as well as of the anthology *Mirabilis*.

There is hope that these high-sounding statements will be followed by further literary activities, if only . . .

---

[4] The essay, a survey of successive generations since 1935/36, had been intended as a lecture to be given in October 1989. It was not delivered, however, due to reasons not disclosed by the author.

APPENDIX A:
SAMPLES OF CONTEMPORARY CAPE VERDEAN WRITING

Precursors of the Independence Generation

Arménio Vieira

Poema

Talvez um dia
Quem sabe! . . .

Sim
talvez um dia. . .
pedra jogada
à nossa gaiola de vidro
e para nós
a fuga
além   fronteira do mar.

Talvez arrebente um dia
o búzio dos mistérios
no fundo do mar
e mais um vulcão venha à tona
—dez vinte
mil vulcões—Quem sabe! . . .
e as ilhas fiquem derretidas:
Estranha alquímia
de montes e árvores
de lavas e mastros
de gestos e gritos.

Talvez um dia
onde é seco o vale
e as árvores dispersas
haja rios e florestas.
E surjam cidades de aço
e os pilões se tornem moínhos.
Ilhas renascidas
nuvens libertas. . .
Talvez um continente
à medida dos nossos desejos.

Sim
talvez um dia. . .
Quem sabe!

Mákua 1. Antologia poética. Sá da Bandeira,
Publicações Imbondeiro, 1962, pp. 21–22.

Poem

Maybe some day
Who knows! . . .

Yes
maybe some day . . .
a stone will smash
our glassy cage
and we shall take
flight
beyond the frontier of the sea.

Maybe some day the conch
shall burst its mystery
deep down in the sea
and one more volcano shall surface
—ten twenty
a thousand volcanos—who knows! . . .
the islands shall melt:
A strange amalgam
of mountains and trees
of lavas and masts
of gestures and screams.

Maybe some day
where the valley is dry
and the trees are sparse
streams and woods shall appear.
Iron cities shall rise
and our pestles turn into mills.
Reborn isles
unleashed clouds . . .
Maybe a continent
at the scale of our dreams.

Yes
maybe some day . . .
Who knows!

Prefácio a um livro futuro
Para C. Valcorba

> La poésie ne rhythmera plus l'action;
> elle sera en avant.

Em dezembro reparei na ortografia
da velha poesia utilitária
e vi que em janeiro
podia começar a dispor as pedras do alfabeto
em sentido oposto ao que até aí
não ultrapassara os limites
de uma nojenta gastronomia poética

Risquei de A a Z os versos úteis
e, numa guerra aberta aos ortopoemas,
decidi que ser poeta a sério
implicava uma espécie de suicídio

Sobre os meus poemas transitivos
tracei uma grande cruz vermelha.

Post Scriptum: Setembro dói e sangra

Em dezembro escrevi o tal prefácio
a um livro futuro. No entanto,
queimado o endereço e morto o lume,
é meu ainda o que dói no verso
e o mais que na alma é gume e sangra.

Arménio Vieira, *Poemas 1971–1979.*
Lisbon, África Editora, 1981, pp. 104–105.

Preface For A Future Book
For C. Valcorba

> Poetry will no longer versify action;
> it will precede.

In December I noted the approved spelling
of the old utilitarian poetry
and I saw that in January
I could start moving the alphabet dominoes
in a direction opposite to the one
which until then did not lead beyond the limits
of a sickening cuisine for poets

I crossed out the useful verses from A to Z
and in open warfare on all the orthodox poems,

I decided that being a poet in earnest
meant committing a kind of suicide

On my transitive poems
I traced a large red cross.

Postscript: September Hurts and Bleeds

In December I wrote that preface
for a book to come. However,
when the address was burnt and the fire gone out,
what hurts in my verse is still my wound
and what else has an edge and bleeds in my soul.

Isto é que fazem de nós

> Isto!

E perguntam-nos:
> — sois homens?

Respondemos:
> — animais de capoeira.

Dizem-nos:
> — bom dia.

Pensamos:
> lá fora. . .

Isto é que fazem de nós
quando nos inquirem:
> — estais vivos?

E em nós
as galinhas respondem:
> — dormimos.

ISTO É QUE FAZEM DE NÓS

> Arménio Vieira, *Poemas 1971–1979.*
> Lisbon, África Editora, 1981, p. 11.

This Is What They Do To Us

> This!

And they ask us:
> "are you human?"

We answer:
> "cooped-up animals."

They say to us:
> "good morning."

We think to ourselves:
> out there . . .

This is what they do to us
when they question us:
> "are you alive?"

And the chickens in us,
the chickens answer:
> "we're asleep."

THIS IS WHAT THEY DO TO US

Histórias recuperadas: as coisas deste mundo e do outro

Mais tarde, depois do incidente, convenci-me de que o fogão a gás não estava nada bem ali no quarto. Mas nessa noite nenhuma lembrança me alertou contra a presença da botija azul a dois-três metros da minha cama. Deitei-me e adormeci de seguida.

Tudo ia bem no sono, desde a respiração à qualidade dos sonhos. Mas de repente senti-me a sufocar. Comecei a tossir muito e à tosse juntou-se uma espécie de náusea ainda mais intensa e pavorosa do que o enjôo que acomete certos marinheiros de estômago fraco. Despertou-me um impulso de desespero. Quase de rastos e arquejando, abeirei-me duma janela e abri-a com um safanão. A aragem fresca da manhã, sorvida a plenos pulmões, devolveu-me o alento quase perdido. Revigorado, nem precisei de raciocinar muito. Dirigi-me ao fogão e dei três voltas ao comutador do gás, fechando-o.

Sobre a banca de cabeceira encontrei um bilhetinho com estes dizeres: "Há cento e cinquenta anos salvaste-me de morrer afogado. Quis ser grato. Encontrando o gás aberto no teu quarto, fechei-o. Mas doravante, cautela, pois nem sempre me é possível abandonar o Astral para socorrer um amigo." A mensagem não estava assinada.

Durante muito tempo o mistério deu-me voltas à cabeça. Até que um dia a leitura súbita de um livro antigo com uma iluminura ao centro representando o Universo me forneceu a provável solução. Grande parte do que pude então depreender não me convém revelar. Fazê-lo seria expor a minha vida a um perigo maior do que o incidente atrás referido. Todavia, sempre me é possível esclarecer o seguinte: o falecido, embora imbuído da melhor das intenções, havia-se equivocado nisto: quando ele penetrou no quarto o gás estava fechado, mas, por não se ter lembrado que no Astral as coisas funcionam em sentido inverso ao deste mundo, em vez de deixar o comutador de gás como o encontrara, tinha-o rodado três vezes para a esquerda.

Ponto & Vírgula, no. 8, March/April 1984, p. 26.

Retrieved Stories: Things of This World and of the Other

Later on, after the incident, I realized that the gas stove did not really belong in the bedroom. But during that night I did not think of anything that would have warned me against the blue box standing six, seven feet away from my bed. I lay down and immediately fell asleep.

Everything about my sleep was perfect, from my breathing to the kind of dreams I had. But suddenly I felt I was suffocating. I started to cough a lot, and the cough was accompanied by something like a nauseous feeling, more intense and frightening even than the seasickness that befalls certain landlubbers with weak stomachs. A desperate impulse woke me up. Almost crawling on all fours and gasping for breath, I sidled up to a window and pushed it open. Taking deep breaths of the fresh morning breeze, I regained strength I had almost lost. Feeling reinvigorated it did not take me long to gather my thoughts. I headed for the stove and turned the knob three times to turn off the gas.

On the bench at the head of the bed I discovered a slip of paper with these words: "One hundred and fifty years ago you saved me from drowning. I wanted to show you my gratitude. Finding the gas turned on in your bedroom I shut it off. But be more careful from now on, because I am not always able to leave the Astral World to help a friend." The message was unsigned.

For a long time I turned the mystery over and over in my mind. Until one day I happened to read an old book with an illuminated picture on its central pages. Its representation of the universe offered me the likely solution. Much of what I learned from it had better not be revealed. If I did so I would endanger my life more than during the incident I have just described. Nevertheless, I can disclose this much: With the best of intentions, the deceased had committed an error. When he penetrated the bedroom the gas was turned off, but not remembering that in the Astral World everything moves contrary to the way it does in this world, he did not leave the gas knob alone but gave it three turns to the left.

Corsino Fortes

Mindelo

Entre a escuridão
E o silêncio da noite. . .
Amachucado
Entre a morna e o violão
Sonho. . . Mindelo
De mãos apoiadas
Sobre o eco da tua pulsação.

Mindelo
Recanto de sonhadores
De poetas e músicos
De aves sem asas
Voando
Em busca de alvo
Na neblina da noite.

Orvalho de lágrima
Gota de saudade
Alegria escurecida
Pelo negrume da vida.

Mindelo
Tuas pedras são sonhos
Tuas brisas ilusões
Tuas ruas são rios
Por onde deslizam lágrimas
Envoltas em sorrisos.

Mindelo
Ó doce Mindelo morno
De Lua Nascente e Poente
De noite debruçado
Na morna dolente
De poesia encostada
Na esquina da noite.

Mindelo de Luzes
De Pétalas e Prantos
Ó quimera perdida
Ó berço adormecido
        embalado
Dentro de mim!

Boletim dos Alunos do Liceu Gil Eanes,
Mindelo, no. 1, 1959.

Mindelo

Amidst the dark
And the silence of night ... .
Bruised
Amidst *morna* and guitar
I dream . . . Mindelo
Hands held tight
On the echo of your heart.

Mindelo
Refuge of dreamers
Of poets and musicians
Of wingless birds
Flying
Toward an unseen star
In the misty night.

Dew of the eyes
Teardrop of longing
Joy of life dimming
In the bleakness of living.

Mindelo
Your stones are dreams
Your breezes deceptions
Your streets are rivers
Where tears are gliding
Wrapped into smiles.

Mindelo
Oh, Mindelo sweet and mournful
Of a moon rising and setting
In the night hunched over
The *morna* of doleful
Poetry leaning
Against the corner of night.

Mindelo of Lights
Of Petals and Plaints
Oh, chimera escaping
Oh, cradle sleeping
            rocking
Inside myself!

Konde palmanhã manchê

Ó konde
Ó konde palmanhã manchê
Konde note ftcha ftchode
E palmanhã manchê
C'pê plantode na tchon
E terra na coraçon
Konde sangue rasgâ na corpe
Arve de broce aberte
E smente gritâ na rotcha
Tambor de boca verde
E daquel som
Ma quel sangue soldode
Nascê boca
       boca centrode
       boca rasgode
Na roda de sol

Ó konde palmanhã manchê
Sem dsuspère pundrode
Na bandêra de porta
Sem lanterna cindide
Na robe de burre
Pa naufroge de navi
Sem navi quebrode
Na boca de pove
E mar bem olte! brobe!
               dsusperode
Bem quebrâ na Praia Grande
Sês broçe gorde de pecode
E mar bem
Na se luxe
E na se grandèza!
Se mostre
De mar erguide na pêto
Se mapa bronque
Desenhode n'alma
Bem bibê na colónia dnha boca
Tod' aquel negoce dnha sangue ultramarine

Ó konde palmanhã manchê
E Criste bem dsê morada
El bem ta bem
Pa broce direite de Monte Cara
C'se cobe d'enxada
Ma se calçon dril
C'se pê na tchon

Ma se dede quebrode
Bem sentâ
Na pedra radonde dnôs fogon
Sem tchuva na mon
Sem fraqueza na sangue
E sem corve na coraçon

Ó konde
Ó konde palmanhã manchê

Corsino Fortes, *Pão & fonema*. Poema.
Lisbon, Sá da Costa, 1974, pp. 57–58.

When the Morn was Dawning

Oh when
Oh when the morn was dawning
When the night was closing its tent
And the morn was dawning
With our feet set on the soil
And the land in our hearts
When the blood spread in the body
A tree with open arms
And the seed beat on the rock
A drum with a green mouth
And from that sound
Joined to that blood
Was born a mouth
           a mouth centered
           a mouth opened
In the disk of the sun

Oh when the morn was dawning
Without despair suspended
From the transom of the door
Without a lantern lit
Tied to a donkey's tail
For a ship to be wrecked
Without news of its grounding
Spread from mouth to mouth
And the sea oh so high! so wild!
                          desperately
The sea came up on the Big Beach and broke
Their arms bulging with sin's loot
And the sea was coming
In all its pomp
In all its grandeur!

Its full display
Of a sea inflating its chest
Its white map
Traced in its heart
It came to swallow in my colonized mouth
All that business about my overseas blood

Oh when the morn was dawning
And Christ came from his abode
He came he is coming
To the right hand of Mount Cara
With his handle of a hoe
And his trousers of drill
With his feet on the ground
And his broken fingers
He came and sat down
On our hearth of round stones
Without rain in his hands
Without weakness in his blood
Without vultures in his heart

Oh when
Oh when the morn was dawning

A lestada de lés a lés

I
Dos músculos de mar a mar
                À pedra larga da alma
Somos
        Dez rostos de terra crua
        E uma pátria de pouco pão
E não há deserto
    não há ilha nem poço
                Que não vença
Pelo olho vítreo da cabra,
                A lestada de lés a lés
Que ontem devolvendo
                devolvemos hoje
Ao esqueleto verde da história
A carne e a cruz
                do "flagelo"
                flagelado que fomos
                Aqui! Onde
A seca é arma E a fome! desafio
A ilha é vida E a secura! vivência
Amor! que a chuva traga
                A bandeira branca
Da nossa guerra Entre céu & terra
                E
Mesmo que o céu não chova
E o Sol e a Lua
                sejam
        cordas partidas no violão da ilha
Mesmo que a chuva seja esta noiva de usura
Este umbigo
Esta corola de ausência
                Entre a rocha e o rosto
Mesmo
        Que o vento
                vergue
No eixo da terra E nos mastros da alma
Os ossos & séculos de sangue & secura
Mesmo sendo! Já não somos
                Os flagelados do vento leste

II
Que o digam
As colinas de labor Que de longe
        tropeçam
                nos membros
                das sementes vagabundas

Que o digam
Os braços do povo no povoado
E os tambores de pão
                    de pedra & pólen
Que sangram
No pulso das mulheres que juram:
Que de fome! a fome não morra
                    E não morra jamais
No espantalho da sua cruz solarenga
Entre o osso de pão
E o esqueleto das padarias
                    Então!
Os joelhos E cotovelos da ilha
                    Esculpiram
No crânio dos homens! para nunca
A flor carnívora das miragens longinquas
E os portos beberam pela proa
A traça
Dos navios fantasmas
Daquela tragédia sem âncora
E sendo! somos
"Um povo de pé sobre a pedra do drama"
                    Aqui! onde
A acção escreve sobre o pensamento
Modelando a rocha E o resto
Deste cabo
Deste teatro
                    verde de vida

Corsino Fortes, *Árvore & tambor.*
Lisbon, Publicações Dom Quixote, 1986, pp. 121–123.
(Part iii of the poem has been omitted.)

Eastwind From End to End

I
From the muscles tensed from sea to sea
                    To the broad rock of the soul
We are
        Ten faces of raw earth
        And a homeland of few cereals
And there is no desert
                no island nor well
                    unable to conquer
                    The eastwind from end to end

Through the goat's glassy eye
Which we returned yesterday
    and return today
To the green bone heap of history
The flesh and the cross
        of the "scourge"
        scourged as we were
        Here! Where
Drought is a weapon And hunger! defiance
The island is life And dryness is living
Love! May rain bring
    The white flag
Of truce in our war between heaven & earth
        And
Even if heaven does not send us rain
And the Sun and the Moon
        be
           broken strings on the island guitar
Even though the rain be the usury's bride
This navel
This corolla of absence
    Between rock and face
Even
    though the wind
    be bending
The axis of earth And the masts of the soul
The bones & centuries of blood and dryness
Even then! No longer are we
      The eastwind's scourged victims

II
Let them tell it
Those hills of plowing Which from afar
    stumble
        upon limbs
        of truant seedlings
Let them tell it
Those arms of the folk in the parish
And the drums of grains
        of pebbles & pollen
Until they bleed
In the wrists of women cursing
Such starvation! May hunger not die
      And never die
On its scarecrow cross of the landlords
Amidst the bone of bread

And the ribcage of bakeshops
                              So then!
The knees And the elbows of the island
                              chiseled
In the human skull forever
The carnivorous flower of faraway visions
And the harbors drank
The worm
              through the prows
Of the phantom ships
Of that tragic anchorless drama
And continuing to be! we are
"A folk that stands upright on the rock of the drama"
                              Here! where
The plot is writing on the forethought
Shaping the rock And all else
        Of this cape
        Of this stage
                        Green with life

Members of the Independence Generation

José Luís Hopffer C. Almada (*Zé di Sant'y Agu*)

"Permanência"

                                    Para Mito, em amizade

A pedra continua inerte
A noite continua incerta
A loucura continua efémera
O sonho continua eterno
A face da Isabelle continua terna
        retratada num futuro que ainda é túnel e lanterna
A água de cada dia continua térmica
O trópico de Cáncer de olhar posto em Santiago continua
                                    hemisférico
Os insultos no estádio da Várzea continuam esféricos
O amor na prancha da cidade continua desinibidamente
                                    espérmico
A aurora para além dos labirintos da cidade continua
                                    quimérica
O polegar de Tchibita continua cadavérico e ressequido
                        sobre o deserto do seu crânio
Os pedintes continuam elegantemente raquíticos e sentados
                        compõem o réquiem do quotidiano
A ilusão continua verde (do verde lunar das serenatas)
                                    neste país
                de pedras em noites loucas
                de pedras que sonham
                na face da água
                que cancera desde o trópico
                dos insultos dos santos cancelados
                e do amor no polegar
                da
                        ilusão sempre erecta
                        no seu verdejar
                        na aurora do pedinte. . .

                        Voz di Letra, no. 4, July 1986, p. 4.

"Permanence"

                                    For Mito, in friendship

Stone remains inert
Night remains indefinite
Folly remains ephemeral

Dreaming remains eternal
Isabelle's face remains tender
          projected into a future still
                    tunnel and lamp
Day in day out the water remains tepid
The tropic of Cancer staring at Santiago
                    remains hemispherical
In the Várzea stadium insults remain spherical
Sex served on the urban platter remains uninhibitedly seminal
Dawn beyond the urban maze remains chimerical
Tchibita's thumb remains cadaverous and withered
                    on the desert of his pate
The cadgers remain elegantly rickety
                    and seated compose the requiem of
                              each day
Illusion remains verdant (like the verdant moon of serenades)
                              in this country
                    of stones on nights of folly
                    of stones that dream
                    facing the water
                    that carries cancer from the tropic
                    of insults to canceled saints
                    and to love in the thumb
                    of always erect illusion
                    as it greens
                    in the dawn of the cadgers . . .

Evocação: Lenbransas di Arvi

Tardi sa ta lenbra-n otus kuzas: kel Arvi na mei di Prasa, kel Arvi ki era sínbulu di Somada. Sima un sínbulu, alel-ba la, sírkulu verdi dentu di un kuadradu di pedra ku planta. Era kunpridu, y si fodjas ku si ramus, sima spada vejetal, ta djuntaba pa formaba transas o midjor grodis di fodjas un riba di otu, kada bes más pikinoti, ti tchigaba la riba, la undi nos odju di mininu ka ta tchigaba. Kel tenpu kuzas ta parseba más grandi: gentis stranhu, Diministrador, sobradus, pulísias, kalseta'l rua, y Arvis tanbé.

Kel bes ki Somada era un Vila kuazi so di "brankus tera" ku funsionárius, rotchadu na 2 ou 3 ruas, kel tenpu di sinzas di Matu Njenhu, kel tenpu era sima si tudu bida di Vila ta jiraba na volta di Arvi'l Prasa. Ora ki benda, e ta odjada, di lonji, di la di Krus di Piku, di tudu kau ta odjada Arvi'l Somada ta subiba seu; kada dia. Nton, pa Natal era sima un sonhu, dentu'l neboa e ta infetada sima Arvi Natal y prezépiu era nos tudu, ki ta staba y ta viveba baxu di Arvi. Nunka N odja un Arvi Natal ton grandi, y nen ka obi fladu nen di obi nen di odja o nen di imajina. Gentis branku ta tomaba ses karu, dentu'l lus ta sendi, es ta subiba Bolanha, ti tchigaba Krus di Piku o nton kazinha d'águ es ta fikaba la ta oserba Arvi, es tudu maravilhadu y enkantadu ku Arvi y tenperatura di Somada. Y es ta konparaba el ku otus Arvis ki es odjaba la pa Oropa. Nunbris ta kubriba rostu ku kutelus di Piku Ntoni, y sensason era di Natal di invernu. Pamodi Arvi era sipresti más grandi di tudu sipresti Somada. Inda ka konxeda akásia. Arvi'l Prasa era un sipresti. Y gosi N sa ta odja: el oropeu, sima el era, era sínbulu Somada. Más tinha tanbê otus sínbulus. Pur izenplu, tinha Polon di Bentrada, grandi, más largu ki strada, tamanhu firmi na tchon. Mas Polon ta viveba na mei di pés di mangui, di goiaba, di lantuna, di kana. Polon era tropikal, era badiu puru. Polon era Arvi'l tera, enbora sen kunpanheru di rasa, anonser Polon di Njenhu, di Piku y alguns otu.

Talves e pur-isu ki kel garsa ki ta pasaba tudu bokinha tardi riba Somada, nen e ka ta djobeba pa Arvi'l Prasa. E ta pasaba, si piskos stendedu, si odju ragalidu, ku rosto so pa Bentrada y gretas di si Polon. Pamodi, Polon tinha un monti gretas. Kenha ki kreba tchigaba kes gretas tinha ki ten kudadu ku spinhus, gudu, gudu, ki ta kubriba korpu di Polon, la na si pé própri. E sima si Polon kreba so pa Garsa podeba disfrutaba di si grelu, verdi, la riba. Ta fladu ma tcheus rabeladu ku disgrasiadu ta baba sukundi dentu'l Polon. Y es ta bebeba águ'l tchuba ki ta fikaba, anu interu, na bariga'l Polon. Ker dizer, Polon era sima un lapa, más un lapa-planta. Demu, sima ten planta-animal ki ta kumi algen, ki es ta tchoma planta karnívuru, si tanbé ki ten planta-lapa, pa ta sukundi algen. Polon, parse-n, ma ti distinus y sis segredus, e sabe'l más ki tudu algen, ki ta staba la. Y e ta sukundi'l ti oxi inda, dentu'l si odju paradu.

Distinu di Arvi'l Prasa, ku distinu di Polon di Bentrada foi diferenti, sima tantus kuza teve tantus distinu diferenti di ruberas di dentu'l Somada.

Arvi'l Prasa parse-n ma era ja bedju, bedjasku propi, kantu kuzas ben kontise. E pusível ki e nanse ku Somada, pa e po Somada más riba inda, sakedu sima e staba riba Fonti Lima, ku Suduguma, ku Pedra Baru, ku Tchada Gomi.

Pur-isu, kantu tudu konfuson ben tchiga, kel stribilin ki ben muda vida di nos tudu, bedju ku nobu, ku nos-otu, na flor di idadi. Arvi'l Prasa sima ki e simira, e ba ta bira sinzentu. Ninhun fodja ka parse'l más riba tchada kabesa. Arvi sima kre ki el staba di lutu. Bon, kel tenpu Somada ben panhaba tanbê tcheus poera, ku si gentis y si mininus tudu rusu, di tera. Era propi un tristeza odjaba Somada. Ku stribilin, Arvi'l Prasa da na kai. E gengi, ora pa un ladu, ora pa otu ladu. Tudu dia, kelo ki nu ta pasaba pertu di el, nu ta fikaba ta diskuti pa undi ki el al kaíba. Riba Kanbra, ku tudu si majestadi y stórias, ku si kulunas branku inkostadu na si paredi verdi (azul, às-ves) ka ta daba, pamodi Kanbra era bunitu di más. Alen disu, nos sa ta imagina Arvi'l Prasa ta kai riba di nobus otoridadi, ku Delegadu di Guvernu y tudu? Y si tinha un kumisiu era modi? O un riunion inportanti? Mesmu tikel munumentu di Infanti, undi nu ta xintaba pa nu dimiraba Kanbra, staba sen si Infanti. Às-ves nu ta sakedaba dianti kanterus di jira-sol, nu ta fikaba ta djobe Kanbra. Y às-ves nu ta faseba futugrafia pretu y branku, nos rostu raganhadu dianti'l verdi'l Kanbra. Nton, nu po na na nos kabesa ma Arvi tinha ki kai o riba varanda kureiu o riba kintal di kaza Djon di Baru. Koitadu varanda kureiu, la ki nu brinkaba tantus kuza, nu brigaba, nu fazeba el kadia di mininu y tchon di liberdadi ku brinkaderas, nu oserbaba minininhas ta pasia na Prasa. La ki nu ta ngataba nós mininensa y nu namora nós primeru bes. Más nos nu kria, y el e bira kada bes mas bedju, ku si tedjas stendedu y si skada di simentu antigu.

Nton, pa nos era distinu: tudu bedjisa ta disapariseba: Arvi'l Prasa, brankus tera, varanda kureiu, y so ta fikaba nos nostalgia di infansia, y otus kuzas, ki al binha. Sima ki e pa mostraba forsa'l distinu, gentis bedju bira ta mori un tras di otu. Sima gentis ba ta mori (kuazi nos tudu nu bira senpai dentu'l Somada), kel mujer di bida ta binha, ku si korpu kabadu y palavras tcheu sobri kau di tudu kuzas ben kai, tudu dentu'l vontadi di Dios, ki al benba faseba djustisa.

Más kel dia, bendu. Bendu y fladu: "Nu sa ta ben korta Arvi'l Prasa." Tudu algen djunta, Prasa intchi di povu ku mininus, fikadu so ta odjadu Arvi'l Prasa ta kortadu. Fase so un rabulisu. Prasa fika el-so, baziu, sisi, sen planta, feiu, sen Natal, xeiu tera, xeiu puera. (. . .)

Nos speransa era kel-otu Arvi'l Prasa, ki nu plantaba na kau, la pundi kel Arvi—kel di Natal ku gentis branku, ku Somada antigu—staba. [. . .] Gentis branku más antigu ben dexa di ta izisti, enbora a-la kazas ku bedjus, branku ku pretu, ku klaru ku sukuru, tudu xintadu dentu'l Somada. Arvi sa ta kria, ta sonbra otus gentis, ki e gentis riku, ku skola, ku kursu o rekursu, y otus mininus, ki ka kre brinka Pulísia-ladron más. Somada gosi e kuazi sidadi. Gentis ta fla ma e sa ta spera so Arvi kria, pa ten tanbê si sínbulu, di sidadi, di Natal ku akasia y jirasol.

Distinu di Polon e más paradu. El kontinua dentu'l Bentrada, kunpridu y largu, sima sempri. So kel garsa ki nunka más ka odjadu. Ta fladu, ma afinal garsa ta pasaba riba'l Somada so pa e xintiba tcheru di Arvi'l Prasa. Polon, era sima si rapariga, sima si puta—lugar di diskansu y di pasa sábi diskansadu, lugar di konsolansa. Ku koperativa ki ben kriadu, ku kampones y fidjus di kampones ku odju abertu, Polon ale-l la, sakedu sima fidjus tera.

Polon ale-l la, na fundu Bentrada. Kre ora ki e ben bedju, ki e durbadu, ta ben ten otu Somada, y ta plantadu otu Polon di Bentrada, pa kel-otu Somada ku se ruberas?

> Praia, 13 di Agostu di 1986, rabespa di Nosa Sinhora da Grasa.
> *Fragmentos*, nos. 5/6, November 1989, pp. 71–72.

Memories of a Tree: An Evocation

The evening is bringing back memories: that Tree in the middle of the Square, that Tree, which was the symbol of Assomada, our town. Like a symbol it stood there, a green circle within a paved square. It was tall, its needle-studded branches forming something like a vegetal sword, twined into braids or rather grids of needles one above another, grids whose size diminished more and more as they rose up to the top where our childish eyes could not reach. Everything seemed bigger in those days, and a lot looked strange to us: the district commissioner, houses with an upper floor, the policemen, paved streets, and the Trees, too, in those days. When Assomada was a town of white folk only, a place for government officials, split sideways along two or three streets, in those days. Mato Engenho lay in ashes; in those days it was as if life centered wholly in the Tree on the Square. Well, a person coming and looking from a distance, from beyond the Cross of the Peak, he would see the Tree of Assomada all the way, rising to the sky, day after day. At Christmastime, well, it was like a dream; amidst the mist it stood, decorated like a Christmas tree, and all of us were the manger scene, standing alive under the Tree. Never have I seen such a big Christmas tree, nor have I ever heard anyone tell of one like it, either from hearsay or having actually seen one with his own eyes, let alone imagined it. The white folk used to take their cars, turn on the headlights, drive up through Bolanha until they got up to the Cross of the Peak, or else to the water tower. Once there, they would park and all of them observe the Tree, dazzled and delighted by the Tree and the temperature of Assomada. And they compared it to other Trees they had seen over there in Europe. When clouds were covering the face and ridges of Antonia Peak it gave one the sensation of a wintery Christmas.

In fact, the Tree was the biggest cypress of all in Assomada. Acacias were not known yet. The Tree on the Square was a cypress. And I can see it now: being European, it was the symbol of Assomada. But there were other symbols besides. For example, there was the Kapok tree of Bentrada, a big one, wider than the road, covering a broad area. But the Kapok lived among mangoes, guavas, lantanas, sugar cane. The Kapok belonged to the Tropics, it was a pure *Badiu*, that is, a Santiago Islander, the native Tree, though the only one of its race, aside from the Kapoks of Engenho, of the Peak, and a few more.

Perhaps that was why the Heron, which at nightfall used to fly over Assomada, never gave a glance at the Tree in the Square. It would pass with its outstretched neck, wide open eyes, its head pointed straight toward Bentrada and the clefts of the Kapok. In fact, the Kapok had a lot of clefts. Whoever wanted to reach those clefts had to watch out for thorns, sharp as sharp can be, which covered the trunk of the Kapok down to its feet. As if the Kapok wanted only the Heron to enjoy its green shoots up on top. It was said that plenty of "rebels," as well as other wretches, went to hide inside the Kapok. And that they would drink the rainwater that remained the year round in the Kapok's belly. I mean the Kapok was like a cave, but a caveplant. What the dickens, as there are animal-plants which eat living beings—they call them carnivorous plants—there also are cave-plants that hide them. When it comes to destinies and their secrets, the Kapok, it seems to me, knows more about them than anyone living there. And it hides them yet today, within its cavernous eye.

The destinies of the Tree on the Square and of the Kapok of Bentrada were to be different, just as there are as many different destinies as there are things in Assomada.

The Tree on the Square, it seems to me, was old already, even ancient, when things started to happen. Possibly it had been born at the same time as Assomada, the places around and even above Assomada also, so firm did it stand above Fonte Lima, Suduguma, Pedra Barros, Achada Gomes.

When therefore all the trouble[1] occurred, when that hullabaloo came it changed every life, old and young, including ours in the bloom of youth. The Tree on the Square seemed to be withering, it was turning ashen. Not one needle sprouted on top of its head anymore. The Tree seemed to want to mourn. Well, in those days Assomada also used to get a lot of dust; its people and their children all looked purple from the color of the earth. Assomada was a sad sight really. Simultaneously with the hullabaloo, the Tree on the Square began to fall. First it leaned to one side, then to the other. Every day, whoever among us passed nearby would argue where it might fall. On the Townhall in all its majesty and traditions, its white columns standing out against its green (at other times blue) walls? That couldn't be; it was just too pretty. Besides, could we imagine the Tree on the Square falling on the new magistrates, the police chief and all the rest? And if a committee was in session what sort of behavior would that be? Or an important meeting? As for the monument to Prince Henry the Navigator, where we used to sit and admire the Townhall, the Prince was missing. Sometimes we would stand still in front of the sunflower beds; we would look at the Townhall. And sometimes we

---

[1] Probably an allusion to the colonial rebellions beginning in 1961.

would take black and white pictures of our grinning faces before the green Townhall. Then we would get it into our heads that the Tree had to fall either on the gallery of the post office or into João de Barros's courtyard. Poor post office gallery, where we used to play all those games, fight, use it as a lockup for the tots and as the "safe" place in games, and from where we would watch the girls walk in the Square. It was there that our age group gathered and first made love. But we grew up, and the gallery became more and more worn with its protruding tiles and its cement steps.

So then, that's what destiny meant to us: everything old would disappear, the Tree on the Square, the native-born white folk, the post office gallery. And what would be left would be nostalgia for our childhood and what went with it. As if destiny wanted to show its force, the old people died in turn, one after another. As people were dying (almost all of us became fatherless in Assomada), that bitch with the wasted body would come and talk a lot about how in the end everything shall fall, wholly according to God's will, who would come to mete out justice.

But on a certain day, *they* had come. They had come and had said: "We have come to cut the Tree on the Square." Everyone gathered. The square filled with the people and their children. They had only stayed to watch the Tree on the Square being cut. All they did was mill around. What was left was the mere square, empty like that, without greenery, ugly, without a Christmas, lots of dirt, lots of dust. (. . .)

Our hope was the other Tree on the Square, the one we would plant at last, where the former Tree, the Christmas Tree of the white folk and old Assomada had been. (. . .)

The oldest white folk would disappear, although there would be houses with old people, whites together with blacks, the light-skinned and the dark-skinned, all living within Assomada. The Tree would grow, it would give shade to other folk, well-off folk who had gone to school, had graduated, had resources. And there would be other children, who would not want to play at cops and robbers anymore. Assomada would actually be a city. Folks were saying that they were just waiting for the Tree to grow, so they would have their own symbol of a city, of a Christmas with acacias and sunflowers.

The Kapok's destiny was more uneventful. It continued to stand in Bentrada, tall and wide as always. Only that heron was never seen again. They say that it had finally flown over Assomada just to smell the Tree on the Square. The Kapok had been like its girl, its broad—a place to rest and have a good time while resting, a comfort. Now that a cooperative had been created and the eyes of the farmers and the farmers' sons had been opened, the Kapok still stood there, firm as the natives.

Look at it standing there, the Kapok, in the heart of Bentrada. Did it now believe that it was quite ancient, that it was confused, would there be a different Assomada, and would a different Kapok of Bentrada be planted for that different Assomada with its neighborhoods?

> Praia, August 13, 1986, on the eve of the Feast of Our Lady of Grace.

Editorial

O ano de 1986 entrará, indubitávelmente, na história da literatura caboverdiana como o ano das maiores dinâmicas culturais vividas no país, desde sempre e, particularmente, desde a independência nacional. [. . .] Referimonos, primeiramente, à criação do Ministério da Cultura e a realização do Simpósio sobre a literatura e a cultura caboverdianas organizada pela Fundação Amílcar Cabral, por ocasião do 50° aniversário da revista *Claridade*, o qual congregou em torno das raízes do nosso ser, a maioria dos homens de cultura caboverdianos (velhos, menos velhos/ menos jovens, jovens). Referimo-nos sobretudo à fundação na cidade da Praia, do Movimento Pró-Cultura em Março. A fundação do Movimento Pró-Cultura contribuiu decisivamente para uma viragem no estado de letargia em que se encontrava mergulhada a literatura caboverdiana e ficará, cremos, consignada como significativa em quatro [*sic*] aspectos: a) Pela primeira vez na história da cultura caboverdiana pós-independência jovens literatos (de parceria com músicos, artistas plásticos, etc.) criaram por sua iniciativa e sem tutela de nenhuma entidade oficial ou oficiosa, uma organização própria, gerida por jovens e com objectivos relativamente ambiciosos. b) A criação do novo movimento resultou do esforço de dinamizadores de diferentes regiões do pais e ocorreu na cidade da Praia, o que significa que é a primeira vez que surge um amplo movimento literário cultural na ilha de Santiago que, embora sendo lugar de nascimento e de laboração de vários grandes literatos caboverdianos, caracteriza-se tradicionalmente pela preponderância da literatura oral e por uma certa incipiência (aliada a um incompreensível mal-estar) no que respeita a movimentações literárias conjuntas. c) Para além de ter permitido que diferentes vertentes culturais comungassem, ainda que experimentalmente, do mesmo ideal de renovação e ensaiassem formas de laboração conjunta, a criação do Movimento Pró-Cultura determinou o surgimento de uma nova geração literária caboverdiana, homogénea na sua generosidade, plural nos seus propósitos, diversa na sua escrita e convicta de si mesma. (. . .)

A geração literária nascida com o Movimento Pró-Cultura revelou-se, essencialmente, no "Voz di Letra," sendo ela tributária de anteriores iniciativas e estando a sua colaboração actualmente dispersa por várias publicações com vertentes literárias ("Voz di Letra," "Seiva," "Sopinha do Alfabeto," "Tribuna" etc.).

O facto de, actualmente, existirem vários grupos de certo modo criaturas (passe o termo) do Movimento Pró-Cultura inicial, nomeadamente o Movimento Pró-Cultura (que publica a revista "FRAGMENTOS") e o grupo coordenador de debates sobre a arte (editor da "Sopinha do Alfabeto") e vários independentes, se por um lado atesta da grande e insofismável vitalidade da nova geração, por outro lado comprova da lamentável insuficiência do espírito de associativismo, [. . .] a par da comprovada necessidade de uma maior informalidade na condução de movimentos literários, da inadiabilidade do diálogo e do pluralismo entre as correntes e da evidente cumplicidade entre os diversos protagonistas, para além de tudo. (. . .)

Enquanto não for fundada a Associação dos Escritores Caboverdianos, deve-se, cremos, pelo menos, fomentar o intercâmbio entre as diferentes publicações existentes (incluindo o "Aurora" e o "Ponto & Vírgula"). [. . .] É neste contexto que vem a lume, neste ano de "Odju d'Águ," a revista "FRAGMENTOS." Revista que queremos aberta, constituindo um verdadeiro e vivo espaço de diálogo entre as diferentes formas de arte, oficinas e gerações. [. . .]

A prossecução dos objectivos supra-dissecados não será decerto possível se não formos uma voz crítica face à nossa sociedade e à sua complexidade ou não cometermos, permanentemente, o suicídio indispensável à isenção da voz e do gesto, com o olhar posto sobre as incongruências do quotidiano.

No que se refere ao conteúdo temático da revista optamos pelo equilíbrio entre os géneros: A poesia, a ficção, o drama, o ensaio (pela sua potência científica, teórica e desmistificadora), a crítica, etc, merecerão igual carinho da nossa revista de Literatura, Arte e Cultura. [. . .]

Fragmentos, no. 1 (August 1987), pp. 3–4.

Editorial

The year 1986 will undoubtedly leave its imprint on the history of Cape Verdean literature as the year of the country's greatest cultural dynamism ever, particularly since national independence. [. . .] We are referring in the first place to the creation of a Ministry of Culture and to the Symposium on Cape Verdean literature and culture organized by the Amilcar Cabral Foundation to commemorate the 50th anniversary of the review *Claridade*. The Symposium brought together most of the personalities contributing to Cape Verdean culture (the old, the not so old/the not so young, and the young), in order to ponder the roots of our existence. We are referring above all to the Pró-Cultura Movement, founded last March in the city of Praia. It was a decisive contribution to rousing Cape Verdean literature from a state of lethargy and will, we believe, be considered significant because of four [sic] aspects:

a) For the first time since independence young literati (in partnership with musicians, practitioners of the plastic arts, etc.) took the initiative to create an organization of their own, free from any official or officious tutelage and directed by the young with relatively ambitious objectives.

b) The creation of the new movement was due to the efforts of activists from different parts of the country, and it occurred in the city of Praia. That means an ample literary and cultural movement arose on Santiago Island for the first time, an island traditionally characterized by a preponderantly oral literature and a certain inexperience (combined with incomprehensible uneasiness) concerning joint literary enterprises, in spite of the fact that several great Cape Verdean writers were born on Santiago and worked there.

c) Beyond allowing different cultural tendencies, at least as an experiment, to share the same ideal of renewal and try out ways of working together, the creation of the Pró-Cultura Movement determined the rise of a new generation in Cape Verdean literature, with homogeneous generosity, plural goals, diverse styles of writing, and filled with self-confidence. [. . .]

The literary generation born with the Pró-Cultura Movement essentially revealed its existence in "Voz di Letra," while owing something to previous initiatives. At present, its contributions are dispersed among several publications with literary tendencies ("Voz di Letra," "Seiva," "Sopinha do Alfabeto," "Tribuna," etc.)

Several groups exist presently, which in a certain way are the offspring (if we may use the term) of the initial Pró-Cultura Movement: the Pró-Cultura Movement itself, which publishes the review FRAGMENTOS, the group coordinating debates on art, which edits "Sopinha do Alfabeto," and several independent ones. On one hand this fact attests to the undeniably great vitality of the new generation. On the other it shows a regrettable dearth of associative spirit. [. . .] At the same time it points to a proven need for greater informality in the conduct of literary movements, the urgency of dialogue and pluralism among the currents, and an obvious complicity among the various protagonists, more than anything else. [. . .]

As long as no Association of Cape Verdean Writers exists one ought at least to encourage an exchange between existing publications, including "Aurora" and "Ponto & Vírgula," we believe. [. . .]

Such is the context in which the review FRAGMENTOS is seeing the light of day this year, the year of the publication of *Odju d'Águ*. We want it to be an open forum for a true, lively dialogue among different art forms, workshops and generations. [. . .] Our conviction that ostracism and rootlessness are two sides of the same alienating and retrograde coin leads us to take our stand in favor of the dialogue between cultures.

It surely will not be possible to pursue the objectives we have detailed above unless we are a critical voice confronting our society in its complexity or commit the ongoing suicide required from a voice and gesture if they are to be unprejudiced when one looks at the incongruities of daily living.

As to the thematic contents of the review we opt for a balance between genres: Poetry, fiction, drama, essayism (because of its scientific, theoretical and demystifying potentialities), criticism, etc., will deserve equal care on the part of our review of Literature, Art and Culture. [. . .]

Tomé Varela da Silva

Ĵa ĉiga ténpu

Nu fase'l korda!
Nu fase'l subi!

Kauberdi ĵa bu durmi ĉeu:
Ti nos séklu kinzi
bu durmi na mar.
Es diskubri-bu
bo bu ka korda.

Ĉuputada palmada:
bo bu ka korda!
Es violenta-bu korpu
bu alma tanbe:
bu ka deŝa durmi!
Bo éra un virĵi:
es fase-bu fiĵus:
bo bu ka korda!

Bu dota bu fiĵus
bu da's bu kariñu:
sénpri na kadia.
Sénpri na tristéza
bu suste bu fiĵus
sen ki bu korda!
Bo bu mamanta's
bo bu aduka's
mas bu ka korda!

Bu da's bu miĵu
kaĉupa ku karni
fiŝon ku toŝiñu.
Tenterén kamóka
masa ku galiña
kuskus ku leti.
Papa ku mantega
kuskus ku mel:
bo bu ka korda!

Bu fiĵus kume
bebe durmi.
Bu fiĵus korda
bisti laba.
Bu fiĵus brinka
trabaĵa kansa.
Bo bu ka korda!

Goiaba laranẑa banana
mangi ẑanbri mamun.
Mandióka ku karni batata
ku peŝi mandióka ku leti.
Kana pa ñeme kalda
pa bebe grógu pa kenta.

Bu fiĵus goza kanta:
bu oĵu k'abri!

Ŝuveru k'abri
bu korpu seka:
bu fiĵus ĉora!
Boi lamenta
kabra pidi
kabalu móre!

Bu fiĵus duense
móre fuŝi.
Ningen ka konŝe'u
tudu kre-bu ĉeu:
bu ten ki korda!
Peŝi ĉeu na mar
galiña na matu
makaku na róĉa.
Sal na mar pa tra
masapé ta dana
praia pa splora.
Viñu pursulana
kal kafé siméntu:
tudu ta spéra!

Bu fiĵus e speransa:
ĵ'es spéra ĉeu:
bu ten ki korda!

(. . .)

T.V. da Silva, *Kumuñon d'Áfrika. Onti oŝi mañan.*
Praia, Instituto Caboverdiano do Livro, 1986,
pp. 61–63.

The Time Had Come

They made us wake up
They made us rise!

Cape Verde, you had slept aplenty:
Until our fifteenth century
you slept in the sea.
They discovered you
You did not wake up!

Beatings ferule slaps:
You did not wake up!
They violated your body
your soul as well:
you did not stop sleeping!
You were a virgin:
they made you bear their children:
you did not wake up!

You adopted your children
you gave them your affection!
all the time in prison.
All the time in sorrow
you sustained your children
without ever awakening!
You nursed them yourself
You brought them up by yourself
but you did not wake up!

You gave them your cornmeal
corn soup with meat
beans with salt pork.
Popcorn sweet potatoes
noodles with chicken
corncake with milk.
Porridge with butter
corncake with honey:
you did not wake up!

Your children ate
drank slept.
Your children woke up.
They dressed they washed.
Your children played
worked got tired.
You did not wake up!

Guavas oranges bananas
mangoes jambos papayas.

Cassava with meat potatoes
with fish cassava with milk.
Sugarcane to chew cane juice
to drink rum to get warm.

Your children had fun they sang:
Your eyes did not open!

No shower opened
your dried-out body:
your children cried!
The oxen bellowed
the goats begged
the horses died!

Your children fell ill
died fled.
Nobody recognized you
all loved you dearly:
you had to wake up!

Lots of fish in the sea
fowls in the bush
monkeys on the rocks.
Salt to take from the sea
black soil going to waste
beaches to exploit.
Wine pozzolana
lime coffee cement:
Everything is waiting!

Your children and hope:
they have already waited aplenty:
you have to wake up!

(. . .)

Natal

Ómi ĵa staba ku si korénta y tal anu riba, na korpu. Éra un grandi solteron y un karpinteru ki si ofisiu ta daba-el so pa pon di kada dia. E' ta pensaba na fase tudu si bida solteru. Mas, komu e' ka tenba ningen, e el ki éra di karpintaría, di paña agu, di kusia, di laba ropa, di muda kabras, di trata di porku ku galiña, di bari kasa. Nen e' ka tenba ténpu di faseba kama.

E pur isu k'el, apénas ku korénta y ĉeu anu, e' sa ta parseba ĵa moradu na sasénta! Óras k'el ŝintaba, e' ka ta labantaba sen ui-ui-ui!

Un dia, dipos ki ĵa pasaba ĉeu ténpu, sen ténpu di fase barba, e' pega si nabaĵa barba, e' po sabon na róstu, e' bai pa speĵu. Nton, e' spanta ku si kabésa, ti ki nabaĵa kai'l di mo. E' kóre mo na kabélu ku na barba, e' puŝa péli nrugadu di piskós; e' ĵobe si brasu, e' diĵiĵi kabésa, e'fla:

— Paĵeĵi, mós, kabu sta'u mau! . . . Ken ki ta fla ma bu ten so 48 anu? . . . Pa ĵa bu sta béĵu si? ! . . . Ki bida e di bo, Paĵéĵi? . . . Bo so riba mundu, sen ningen di oĵa pa bo n'es beĵisa li! . . .

Nton, e' skese m'el tenba róstu tudu nsabuadu. E' rabida, e' ŝinta riba di un kaŝóti, e' diskansa kutubélu ndreta na pónta dueĵu y keŝada na palmu mo, e' diskansa mo skérda na koŝa, e' fika ta pensa si bida, ta matuta mundu. Di li un bokadu, kantu ĵ'el staba skesedu di ténpu y di si afazer, e' labanta, e' da palmu — uaki! —, e' fla:

— Tardi e miĵor ki nunka! . . . So kasa k'e ramédi. . . Bu ten ki kasa, Paĵéĵi! . . . Y ten ki ser ẑa, pamodi sinon, sima beĵisa ĵa lansia na bo li, niñun muĵer ka ta meste-bu. . . . Es ta fla'u: «Kasa ku ño e kasa ku mórtu!»

Anton, e' ba dianti speĵu. E' rapara ma sabon ĵa kaba seka'l na róstu. E' dimira:

— E. . . N staba purparadu pa fase barba! . . .

E' rabida, e' ĵobe nabaĵa riba mésa, e'ĵobe riba kaŝóti, e' purgunta dimiradu:

— Mas, undi ki N po nabaĵa? ! . . .

Nton, e' rabida si, e' oĵa'l na ĉon, si baŝu. E' baŝa p'el paña, e' kudi:

— Ui-ui-ui! . . . Mós, ĵa bu béĵu di tudu manera! . . . Mas, kasa go, bu ten ki kasa, y ẑa!

E' torna po sabon na róstu y, inkuantu e' sa ta barbiaba, e' ba ta kóre ku ŝintidu, p'el diskubri keña ki ta sérba si muĵer. Ĵ'el kaba barbia, ĵ'el linpa róstu, é' sa ta guardaba nabaĵa, kantu e' ragala oĵu, e' fla dimiradu:

— Bia? ! . . . Mas, Bia pode ser ña nétu prontu! . . . E feiu pa mi ku kuazi 50 anu, pa N kasa ku un raparigiña di 16 anu! . . . Na. . . kel li própi! . . . Mo' ki ta fladu? ! . . . Bon. . . mas tanbe si bo béĵu, bu ba kasa ku béĵu. . . e dos sangi friu! . . . Mininiña si debe sperta un ómi sangi na korpu! . . . E si própri! . . . Si kre papiadu. . . Si Bia ĵa kre, mi, N ka sta li! . . . Y si Bia ka kre?! . . . E' pode pensa: «Mi, un raparigiña nóbu si, pa N ba kasa ku ómi béĵu?» Na. . . e' ta kre, sin! Bia e un raparigiña spesial mé, mas raparigiñas di gósi sta tudu ku gana kasa! Sertéza k'el ta seta ña propósta di kasamentu!

Anton, e' toma si bon bañu, e' pentia si kabélu, e' skoĵe si miĵór kalsa ku kamisa, e' bisti, e' kalsa si sandaja di kori, e' da rinkada p'el ba papia ku Bia. Mas, kantu e' ta fiĉa pórta, e' fla pa si kabésa:

— Oŝi, pelu ménus, inkuantu bu sta ku Bia, bu ten ki skese di bu dór! . . . Nada di ui-ui-ui!

Bia moraba un bokadiñu afastadu, mas na si rubera. E' bai ku sórti: e' aĉa Bia na rubera, ki bai paña agu na fonti! E' da'l «bon dia», e' ba pa el, e' stende'l mo. Bia stende'l mo, fla'l:

— Ñu da-m benson, ñu Pajéji!

Pajéji, tudu transtornadu, ragala oju, fla'l:

— O Biaziña. . . ka bu toma-m benson di zimóla! . . . Mi, N stende-bu mo pa nu perta kunpañéru! Mi e solteru sima bo. . . libri sima bo. . .

Bia, nton, fika ŝeiu di burgóña, pur kazu di kel si nganu. E' ka aĉa nada di fla, sinon un grasiña di kebra nbarasu ki ta ividensiaba mas si nbarasu. Pajéji ki ntende kel situason, pega'l na mo, arma perta'l si na si brasu, fla'l, omésmu ténpu k'el ta konkoba Biaziña na ónbru:

— Ka ten nportansa. . . ka ten nportansa! . . . Ža góra, deŝa N fla-bu kus'e ki fase-m ben kontra ku bo gósi. . . N ben fla-bu ma N kre-bu pa bu kasa ku mi, y ma N kre bu raspósta sértu, pamodi kasamentu e dentu ža! Ña konbérsu e klaru, kran-kran, pamodi ža N ka sta rapasiñu. . .

Bia da burgóña, po róstu d'un banda y oju na ĉon. Pajéji fla'l:

— O Biaziña! . . . Burgóña pa k'e y pa k'e pensa ĉeu? . . . Ña propósta e klaru sima agu di kel fonti li, y ña sentimentu ten ónra di ñas idadi y ñas trabaju. . .

— Mas, mi inda e ton nóbu. . .

— Kel la ka ta fase nada. Bo bu ta da-m bu sangi nóbu y bu freskura di žuventudi. . . mi, N ta da-bu ña kariñu y ña spiriénsa di algen ki ža vive!

— Ñu spéra N ta ba fla na kasa purmeru. . .

— Purmeru, ka bu fla-m «ño», mas trata-m sima N ta trata-bu. . . Nos e dos solteru. Sugundu, ki tene bu sentimentu, e ka bu pai ku bu mai. . . E bo própi! Bo k'e dónu di bu kabésa. . . di bu distinu! Sinon, nbes di N papia ku bo, N ta ba papiaba ku bu gentis grandi.

— Diskulpa-m, Pajéji! . . . Kasamentu, tudu mujer kre! Mi inda e nóbu. . . N ten speransa ma si N spéra, ma nt'aĉa ña sórti. . .

— Mas, suguru e na bolsu! . . . Futuru ka sta na mo di ningen. . . Y óras ki ñu aĉa séti, ka ñu spéra kaseti! . . .

— Pajéji, mi, N sta konfuzu! . . . Mas, si vive ku bo e sabi sima bu ta papia, nton ža N kre-bu y mi e di-bo, nen si papái ku mamái ka kre!

Pajéji da un jatu (ka ui-ui, nau!), e' barsa si Biaziña ki barsa'l, na meiu di un grasa. Anton, Pajéji fla'l:

— Si bu aĉa ña papia sabi, mas sabi bu t'aĉa vive ku mi!

Pajéji juda Bia po lata d'agu na kabésa, kunpaña'l kasa, di mo dadu. Kantu es ĉiga kasa, pai ku mai di Bia resebe Pajéji ku grasa na denti, purgunta'l meiu sériu, meiu na brinkadera:

— Ki nobidadi ñu tarse-nu? . . .

— Bon. . . pa N ka anda-ños di róda, nen pa N tene-ños, N ben fla-ños pa ños da-m Biaziña pa kasamentu, ža ki nu kre kunpañéru y ña propósta e sériu!

Pai ku mai abri oĵu, ĵobe kunpañéru. Biaziña sta la kintal na bóltas di kuziña. Mai rusponde:

— E un grandi nobidadi ki nu ka sa ta kontaba ku el! . . .

Pai toma palabra:

— Bon. . . nô ĵa ñu sta un poku madur. . . Rialmenti, ĵa e maré di ñu supara kabésa. . . Mas, Bia e un bokadu nóbu pa ño, sigundu ta parse-m. . . Go, si ĵa nôs kre kunpañeru dretu, y ños ta ntende ku kunpañéru. . . nos nu ka ten kusa fase, sinon seta y dizeźa-ños tudu sórti di mundu!

Poku ténpu dipos, Paĵéĵi ĵa staba kasadu ku si Biaziña. Mas Bia staba un poku diziludidu. Paĵéĵi ĵa ka sa ta aguentaba si nóbu. Len disu, so na ĵuguta pon, ku si karpintaría, albes Bia ta durmiba, ta korda, inda e' ta obiba, o séra ta sera, o martélu ta bate.

Un noti, braźeru di biziñasa ki ĵa notaba kel bida di disgostu sukundidu ki Bia ta lebaba, razolbe prega Paĵéĵi partida y da Bia un poku di filisidadi.

Bia ta deŝaba pórta ngostadu, p'el ka tenba ki labanta, na meiu di si sónu, p'el ba abriba Paĵéĵi pórta, ĵa ki ofisina di Paĵéĵi fikaba na un kasa, na ladu.

Braźeru kel noti, inkuantu Paĵéĵi staba tudu prokupadu na si sera, si plaina y si prega, e' pinĉa pórta ku ĵetu, e' entra, e' aĉa «tabua» di Bia (ki sa ta durmiba sima źustu) ben purparadu. Kantu e' ta da kónta, e' sa ta pregaba manenti, ku tudu furia. Bia korda. La undi el ta grita (di sabura?), braźeru tapa'l mo na bóka, fla'l:

— Fika kétu, bu toma gostu ki tioŝi bu ka ŝintiba!

Sabura éra dimas pa Bia, k'el skese m'el éra kasadu. Na fin, braźeru lolo — iós! —, ba si kamiñu, p'el ka parse nunka mas. Y Bia ka konsigi diskubri keña el éra.

Kantu Paĵéĵi ba deta, Bia staba ta suñaba ku ripitison di kel kusa sabi, mas ku própi Paĵéĵi, ki nen ka rapara si Bia staba na sónu o kordadu. Paĵéĵi, ku si kansera, ántis di korpu ĉiga'l kama, ĵ'el sa ta ronkaba sónu.

Pasa algun ténpu, Bia ŝinti sintómas di preña nóbu. E' da kudadu. So podeba sérba óbra di kel braźeru. Ĵa pasaba mutu ténpu k'el ka ŝintiba ĉeru si maridu. Kantu Paĵéĵi diskubri ma Bia staba preña, e' larga Bia dentu kasa, e' perde uns dia. E' tenba sertéza ma kel gravides éra manifestason di kifri. Entritantu, e' pensa:

— Paĵéĵi, mininu ki Bia tene na bariga e ka di-bo. Mas Bia e di-bo, dos bes pelu ménus. . . E di-bo pa kasamentu y e di-bo pa konsumason di kasamentu! Konsidera go ma bo e pai di Bia y ma si mininu e bu netiñu. . . Ba toma kónta di bu Biaźina ki ĵa ranźa-bu fiĵu ki, kre, ĵa bu ka staba na ĵetu te'l. . .

E' volta pa kasa, e' vive ku si muĵer nobidadi ka ten. Dia 24 di Dizénbru, Paĵéĵi ku si muĵer ba fésta di munisipi na un konseĵu ki fikaba un poku lonźi, apezar di Bia ĵa staba katróŝa. Noti ĵa staba avansadu, kantu dór di pari ĉiga na Bia. Es bate na ĉeu pórta pa da oménus Bia gazaĵu, p'el ka tenba fiĵu na firiésa di rua. Mas, es kaba ku fika na rua. Ramédi ka ten, es buska un kasa limaria, undi es ka mesteba bate na pórta, nen ningen pa gazaĵa's.

Mia-noti di dia 24, nase (ĵuntu ku dia 25) fiĵu di Bia k'era adotivu di Paĵéĵi, entri bóstas di limarias, sura di burus, rinĉa di kabalus, nbera di bakas, kanta di galus. Éra un manera d'es partisipa na indiginason y alegría di kel nasimentu.

Paĵéĵi, indiginadu ku falta di solidariadadi di gentis di kel munisipi y satusfetu ku alegría ki tudu kes limaria manifesta, e' po mininu nómi di Imanuel, ker dizer: «Diós ku nos».

— Mas tardi, Imanuel k'éra mutu spertiñu, kantu e' sabe m'el ka tenba pai (sinon adotivu), e' razolbe fla m'el e fiĵu di Diós ki sa ta sperada, y e' tenta konporta komu tal.

T. V. da Silva, *Natal y Kontus*.
Praia, Instituto Caboverdiano do Livro,
1988, pp. 113–119.

Christmas

The man already carried over forty years on his shoulders. He was a confirmed bachelor and a carpenter by trade earning just enough for his daily bread. He thought he'd remain a bachelor for the rest of his life. But since he didn't have any help, he had to attend to the carpentry shop, fetch water, cook, wash his clothes, move the goats, feed the pigs and the chickens, sweep the house. He didn't even have time to make his bed.

And so it happened that he looked like a man in his sixties, though he was a mere forty-plus years old. Whenever he had been sitting he did not get up without groaning: "Ayayay!"

One day, not having shaved for a long stretch because he hadn't found the time, he got hold of his razor, he soaped his face, he went to the mirror. The way his head looked gave him such a shock that the razor fell out of his hand. He ran his hand over his hair and over his chin, he pulled at the wrinkled skin of his neck, he looked at his arms, he pulled at their wrinkled skin, he shook his head and said:

"Daddy Joe, young man, after all you're that old-looking? ! . . . Who says you're only forty-eight? Already you're that old-looking? ! . . . What kind of a life are you leading, Daddy Joe? . . . You're alone in the world, with no one to look after you in this your old age! . . ."

So he forgot that his face was full of soap. He turned around, he sat down on a box, he rested his right elbow on the cap of his knee and his chin in the palm of his hand, he rested his left hand on his thigh, he kept thinking about his life, he mulled everything over. After a little while, oblivious of the time and of his chores, he got up, he clapped his hands — nevertheless — and he said:

"Better late than never! . . . The only way out is to get married . . . You have to get married, Daddy Joe! . . . And it's got to be right away, if not, no woman will want you, as old age is already here, afflicting you . . . They'll tell you: to marry you, sir, is to marry a dead man! . . ."

So he went before the mirror. He noticed that the foam had already dried on his face. He was amazed:

"That's right . . . I was about to shave! . . ."

He turned around, he looked for the razor on the table, he looked for it on the box, he asked himself with amazement:

"But, where did I put the razor? ! . . ."

He then turned around, he saw it down there on the floor. He bent down to pick it up, the pain gave him the cue:

"Ayayay! . . . Young man, you're already old in every way! . . . But, get married now, you have to get married, and right away!"

Once more he put soap on his face, and while he was shaving, he kept racking his brain to discover who could become his wife. He had already finished shaving, he had already cleaned his face, he was putting the razor away when his eyes opened wide. He said to himself with surprise:

"Mimi? ! . . . But Mimi could be my granddaughter almost! . . . It's unbecoming for me who's close to fifty to marry a sixteen year old babe! . . . Nope . . . A fine thing that would be! . . . The way people would talk? ! . . . Well . . . but you, old fellow, you're going to marry an old woman . . . that'll make two frigid lovers! . . . A little girl like that should arouse a man's blood in his body! . . . That's the proper way! . . . It'll require some talking . . . If Mimi really wants to, I won't stand back! . . . And if Mimi wouldn't want to? . . . She might think to herself: A young babe like me, going to marry an old man? Nope, she'll want to, yessir! Mimi is a special babe indeed, and nowadays the babes are all eager to get married! It's a sure thing that she'll accept my marriage proposal!"

So he took a good bath, he combed his hair, he selected his best pants and shirt, he got dressed, he put on his leather sandals, he sallied forth to go and talk with Mimi. But as he was closing the door, he said to himself: "At least today, while you are with Mimi, you must forget about your aches. No ayayays!"

Mimi lived at some distance, but in the same valley as he. Luck was with him: he found Mimi in the valley, fetching water at the fountain! He bid her good day, he went to her, he held out his hand. Mimi held out hers to him, saying:

"Give me your blessing, Mister Daddy Joe!"

Quite upset, Daddy Joe opened his eyes wide, saying to her:

"Oh, dear Mimi . . . Don't receive my blessing as a charity! . . . I held out my hand to you to shake yours as one partner to another! I am single like you . . . free like you."

Thereupon Mimi was embarrassed by her blunder. She didn't find words, except to make fun of herself in order to dispel the embarrassment, but that made her embarrassment more obvious. Daddy Joe, who realized the situation, took her by the hand, got ready to put his arm around her, talked to her, at the same time that he tapped dear Mimi on the shoulder:

"Never mind . . . Never mind! . . . Now then, let me tell you what has brought me here to look you up today . . . I've come to tell you that

I want you to marry me and that I want your definite response because the wedding will be decided upon right away. I'm talking to you plainly, without beating around the bush because I am no youngster . . ."

Mimi felt ashamed, turned her head aside and cast her eyes down. Daddy Joe said to her:

"Oh, dear Mimi! . . . Why be ashamed and why give it so much thought? . . . My proposal is as clear as the water of this fountain here, and my feelings are as honorable as my age and my labor . . ."

"But, I, I am still so young . . ."

"That doesn't matter a bit. You, you'll offer me your young blood and your youthful freshness . . . I, I'll offer you my affection and the experience of my long life!"

"Sir, wait, I'll first go and talk to my family . . ."

"First of all, don't call me 'sir,' but talk to me as I talk to you . . . Both of us are single. Secondly, it's not a question of your father's feelings or your mother's . . . It's a question of your own feelings! You are the mistress of your mind . . . of your destiny. Otherwise, instead of me talking to you I would have talked to your old people."

"You must excuse me, Daddy Joe! . . . A marriage is what all women want! Me, I'm still so young . . . I have hopes that if I wait for my chance . . ."

"But, better safe than sorry! . . . The future is in no one's hands . . . And when you find a pot of gold, grab it or you'll be left out in the cold! . . ."

"Daddy Joe, me, I'm so confused! . . . But if to live with you is as nice as you say it is, then I'll indeed love you, and I shall be yours, even if dad and mama don't want me to!"

Daddy Joe gave a yell (and it wasn't "ayayay," oh no!), he embraced his dear Mimi, who embraced him, creating a charming scene. Thereupon, Daddy Joe said to her:

"If you find my talk nice, you'll find living with me even nicer!"

Daddy Joe helped Mimi place the water can on her head, he accompanied her home, holding hands with her.

When they reached her house, her father and mother received Daddy Joe with pleasantries on their lips, asking him half seriously, half jokingly:

"What big news did you bring us, sir? . . ."

"Well, not to beat around the bush, and not to keep you people waiting, I have come to tell you, Mr. and Mrs., to give me dear Mimi in marriage, since we want to be partners and my proposal is meant seriously!"

Father and mother made big eyes, looking at each other. Dear Mimi was outside in the yard, busy cooking. The mother replied:

"That's big news, and we didn't expect it! . . ."

The father spoke in his turn:

"Well . . ., sir, you're of a somewhat ripe age already. Really, it's high time you made up your mind, sir. But Mimi is a bit young for you, it seems to me . . . Now, if you two people want the right kind of mate and you understand each other there is nothing we can do but to accept and wish you all the luck in the world!"

A short time thereafter, Daddy Joe was already married to his dear Mimi. But Mimi was a bit disillusioned. Daddy Joe no longer was able to keep up with his young bride. Besides, he would be alone in his carpentry shop, at work for their daily bread, while Mimi was asleep. She would wake up, still hearing him sawing or hammering away.

One night, a mischievous fellow in the neighborhood, who had already noticed the life of secret displeasure Mimi was leading, decided to play a trick on Daddy Joe and give Mimi a little happiness.

Mimi used to leave the door ajar so that she would not have to get up in the middle of her sleep to open the door for Daddy Joe, since his workshop was in a shed beside the house.

That night, while Daddy Joe was wholly absorbed in his work with his saw, his plane and his nails, the mischievous fellow gently pushed the door, entered and found flat-bellied Mimi (who was sleeping the sleep of the just) quite ready. When he realized it, he kept hitting the nail furiously again and again. Mimi woke up. When she screamed (with delight?) the mischievous fellow covered her mouth with his hand and said to her:

"Keep quiet, you have enjoyed what you had never felt until this day!" The delight was too great for Mimi, who forgot that she was married. Gliding away, the mischievous fellow went his way, never to show up again. And Mimi could not find out who he was.

When Daddy Joe went to bed, Mimi was dreaming of a repetition of that delightful business, but this time with Daddy Joe himself, who wasn't even aware whether Mimi was asleep or awake. Tired out, Daddy Joe was snoring sleepily even before his body dropped into bed.

Some time passed. Mimi felt the early symptoms of pregnancy. She worried. It could only be the doing of that mischievous fellow. It had already been a long time since she had smelled her husband's odor. When Daddy Joe discovered Mimi's state he left Mimi alone inside the house. He lost several days. He was sure that the pregnancy signified her having made him a cuckold. However, he thought:

"Daddy Joe, the child in Mimi's womb is not yours. But Mimi is yours twice if not more . . . She is yours by marriage and yours by the consummation of marriage! Suppose now that you are Mimi's father and her child your little grandchild . . . You would take care of your dear Mimi, who had given you a child which, I believe, you were no longer in a condition to beget . . ."

He returned home, he lived with his wife, and nothing untoward happened. On the 24th of December, Daddy Joe took his wife to the festivities in the town of a district that was rather far away, although Mimi was big with child. It was already late at night when her labor pangs began. They knocked on many doors to ask for shelter, at least for Mimi, so that she would not have her child out in the cold street . . . But that's where they ended up, in the street. There was nothing left for them to do but to look for a stable, where they would not need to knock on the door and be refused shelter. At midnight on the 24th, when the 25th was nigh, Mimi's child, whom Daddy Joe adopted, was born amidst the dung of animals, the braying of donkeys, the whinnying of horses, the mooing of cows, the crowing of roosters. It was the animals' way of taking a part in the indignation and the joy over that birth.

Daddy Joe, indignant about the lack of solidarity shown by the people of that town and glad about the joy manifested by all those animals, gave the boy the name Emanuel, which means "God with Us."

But later on, when Emanuel, who was very smart, found out that he did not have a father, only an adoptive father, Daddy Joe decided to tell him that he was the expected son of God, and he tried to behave as such.

Jorge Carlos Fonseca

A matemática da liberdade

Que havíamos de fazer na escuridão rouca da noite de pássaros?
Dormir, esbracejar, entregar as armas?
NÃO, INVENTAR AS PALAVRAS.

Vamos dar o alarme: que nada seja feito sem aviso prévio
(É o paradigma dos sinais de amanhã—a amizade medida em
computadores).

Até saiu um decreto podendo os polícias fabricar poesia!

Ainda por cima era Natal
cheirava a festa as pedras as criaturas as noivas os cadáveres a
bênção do Verbo chovia paz nos corações
os passeios cobertos de pastel de nata
conjugavam o verbo empastar
eu (em) pasto
tu (em) pastas
nós (em) pastamos.

Eram os corredores brilhantes de ciclistas
esvoaçando por entre alas de robots-cinzento pardo
(maravilha desfeita imediatamente com o cheiro das exiladas putrefactas
feitas escarradeira de cavaleiros nocturnos de braçadeira negra).

As ruas alagaram—falta um se senhor professor—de corruptas
com o sangue jovem do produto arrematado na Praça-Prostituta
do quem-mais dá-é quem mais tem.
Falaram de estatística liberdade explosão demográfica inversão de marcha
em tudo.
Somente se esqueceram da ESCOLA TOTAL (necessidade que dizem se
respira)
que poderá matematizar toda a produção seja de queijo seja
de presentes.

Aos ouvintes direi que toda a VERDADE se reduz a
NATAL MAIS ANO NOVO MAIS SUOR MAIS AMANTES MENOS AQUELA MÚSICA
IRRITANTE DAQUELE DISCO ROUBADO NO SUPER É—AMOR-DULCE-DE-TODA-A-
GENTE ponto final

Raízes, no. 1. Praia, January/April 1977, p. 85.

The Mathematics of Liberty

What should we do in the raucous darkness of the birds' night?
Sleep, wave our arms, hand over our weapons?
NO, INVENT WORDS.

Let's sound the alarm: let nothing be done without previous warning
(It's the paradigm of tomorrow's signals—computerized friendship.)

It was even decreed that policemen could fabricate poetry!

On top of that it was Christmastime
    holiday smells exuded from the stones, the living, the brides, the
    corpses the blessing of the Word was showering peace on the hearts
    the sidewalks covered with creamy pasties
        were conjugating the verb "to past(ur)e"
                    I past(ur)e
                 you past(ur)e
                 we past(ur)e
The alleys shining with cyclists
    flitting between rows of ash-colored robots
    (a marvel immediately undone by the smell of the putrefied females
    in exile changed to spittoons for nocturnal riders with black armbands)
The streets were flooded—lacking a professed Professor Doctor—
    corrupted by the young blood of the product auctioned off in the
        Prostitute-Market of "he who gives most is he who has most."

They talked of statistics of liberty population explosion regression in toto.
They only forgot the TOTAL SCHOOL (a need that's in the air as they say)
    which could mathematically express all production be it of cheese or of
                                                            presents.

To listeners I shall say that all TRUTH is summed up in
CHRISTMAS PLUS NEW YEAR PLUS SWEAT PLUS LOVERS MINUS THAT IRKSOME
MUSIC OF THAT RECORD STOLEN FROM THE SUPERMARKET IT'S—SWEET-LOVE-
OF-ALL period

Adelina C. da Silva

Regresso à terra

Estranho me sinto
entre estas rochas nuas
ontem paredes
de um pobre casebre
que foi meu lar.
Passo a passo
nas tuas praias
segue o vulto
de uma criança
que no teu seio
viu a luz.
Oiço um riso,
um murmúrio
vem, toca-me
sente-me
somos um.
O que oiço não é
a voz de antes
sinto perder o laço
que me prendia,
do mar o afago,
do ar o alívio,
do lar a sombra cálida!
Que estranha sensação de filho pródigo!

Arquipélago, no. 9. Boston, May 1988, p. 36.

Return to the Homeland

I feel like a stranger
amidst these bare rocks
only yesterday walls
of a wretched cabin
that had been my home.
Step after step
along your beaches
a child's dim shape
continues walking
which at your breast
saw the light of day.
I'm hearing laughter,
a whisper

come, touch me,
feel me
we're one.

What I'm hearing is not
the voice of yore
the bond that bound me
is slipping I feel it
the sea's tender touches
the breeze bringing coolness
the warm shade of home!
How strange to feel like a prodigal son!

"Alsasem" (Alexandre Sanches Semedo)

Não aceitarei bluff

. . .
Não me hão-de convencer
os donos-da-palavra
(. . .)
alheios da Verdade
observadores míopes
(quando querem)
da verdadeira realidade
da nossa maioria.

1986. Unpublished.

Bluff I Shall Not Accept

(. . .)
They shall not fool me
those whose Word is law
who're not concerned about Truth
who turn a blind eye
(when they want)
to the actual reality
of the vast mass of us.

Pessimismo e anseio

Em jeito de memória de 1985,
Ano Internacional da Juventude.

Dos quatro pontos cardiais
farto
está-se de apregoar
que a Juventude
"é a esperança
e a certeza do futuro"
sem nada de concreto
palpável
para o seu amanhã
superando o hoje
afogada na miséria
guerra
droga
álcool
prostituição
roubo
fome.
(. . .)
Anseia-se
nas sete partidas do mundo
a um raiar verdadeiro
sem mácula
com paciência e perspicácia
pertinência e consequência
(. . .)
renegando o papel
de inconsequente espectador
do desenrolar da História
e contínuo desenvolvimento
(. . .)

1985. Unpublished.

Pessimism and Yearning

> As a remembrance of 1985,
> the International Year of Youth

From the four cardinal points
we're fed up to hear proclamations
that Youth "is the hope, the sure hope of the future"
without concrete evidence
something palpable
to show that tomorrow
shall improve on today
Youth is plunged into misery
war
drugs
alcohol
prostitution
robbery
starvation
(. . .)
There is a yearning
in earth's seven parts
for a real new dawn
without blemish
with action that's patient and provident
pertinent and consequent
(. . .)
No longer content to play
the bystander inconsequentially
watching as History before him unfolds
and constantly marks development
(. . .)

Que Fique Claro!

Dizer
podem dizer
que
os ouvidos são para ouvir
mas
acreditar é outra vertente
meu trunfo
a ser jogado
no último recurso.

Podem
bem apregoar
aos sete ventos
pelas sete-partidas-do-mundo
—é mesmo isso?—
mas
que fique a nu
que
os meus ouvidos
não são lixeiras
para tamanha imundície
causa de tanto pejo.

Que fique claro
para tantas outras
que
os ouvidos são para ouvir
mas
acreditar é outra vertente.

Praia, June 30, 1988. Unpublished.

Let It be Clear!

Talk
they may talk
for
ears are there to hear
but
belief takes a different slant
my trump
to be played
as a last resort.

They may
well harangue
to the seven winds
throughout the seven continents
—is that really so?—
but
know the naked truth
that
my ears
are no dumps
for so much garbage
causing so much trouble.

Let it be clear
as for so many other things
that
ears are there to hear
but
belief takes a different slant.

"Binga" (Alberto Ferreira Gomes)

Tamarindo mártir

> (Aos meus colegas de infância
> particularmente Sabino e Djôdje d'Mitéria)

Debaixo daquele tamarindeiro
Que foi um mártir da seca
Um mártir da estiagem
Como os homens da sua terra

Debaixo daquele tamarindeiro
Que foi massacrado pelas crianças
Que foi massacrado por nós, as crianças
Com cordas para baloiçar
Com pedradas
Com o corte dos rebentos
Com a colheita dos frutos verdes
Sentava-se Mã Djidjula
Tão velha e tão massacrada pelas intempéries da vida
Recebendo a sombra e o aroma do tamarindeiro velho
Velho e curvado e resistente

Mas hoje não existe o tamarindeiro
E nem a Mã Djidjula. . .
O tamarindeiro resistiu à seca
Mas não ao machado manejado pelo homem
Ele foi cortado para cozer a cachupa. . .

E as crianças
Nossas/Minhas sucessoras não têm uma árvore
Não têm uma árvore para lhes dar a sombra
Não têm um tamarindeiro para tirarem os frutos
Não têm uma Mã Djidjula tão velha, tão, boa. . .

A morte levou Mã Djidjula já velhinha
E o homem encarregou-se de levar o tamarindeiro
Tão velho, Tão resistente, Tão forte, Tão bom e Tão. . . Belo. . .

> Luanda, July 1979
> *Aulil*. Ilha do Sal, Município do Sal,
> 1987, pp. 18–19.

The Martyred Tamarind

(To my childhood playmates, especially
Sabino and Demetria's son Georgie)

Under that tamarind tree
A martyr of drought
A martyr of long dry years
Just like its countrymen

Under that tamarind tree
Mistreated by children
Mistreated by us, the children
With ropes to swing on
With stones thrown at it
By breaking its young green shoots
By picking its unripe fruit
Mother Jijulia would sit there
Looking so old and mistreated by life's rough moments
Glad for the shade and the scent of the old tamarind
Old and bent and resistant

But now the tamarind is no more
And Mother Jijulia neither . . .

The tamarind tree that resisted the drought
Was helpless before the man with the axe
Down it went into the fire to cook the *cachupa* . . .
And the children
Who came after us/after me they have no such tree
They have none to give them its shade
They have no tamarind tree to gather its fruit
They have no kindly old Mother Jijulia . . .

Death has taken Mother Jijulia away when she was too old
And man on his own took the tamarind tree
The old tamarind, so resistant, so strong, so good and so . . .
                                                    beautiful . . .

Indecisão

(Para os colegas da Meteorologia)

Não sei, não sei
Se escrever este poema é o ideal
Enquanto a chuva poeticamente
Canta no telhado e acaricia o solo

Não sei
Se o momento é propício
Para colher um poema
Sob a mortiça luz da vela
Enquanto ausente a luz eléctrica

Não sei se
Se devo escutar a chuva
Ou escrever sob o seu ritmo. . .
Acordei-me e a ideia é escrever algo
Nesta chuvosa noite de Setembro

Não sei
Se escrevendo um poema sem rimas
Quebrarei as gotas de água. . .
No cinema o filme foi interrompido
A chuva furiosamente cortou a corrente
   (assim soube pela janela)

Não sei o que hei-de fazer
Em estrondos e ais
Oiço trovões e gritos de jovens
Jovens purificando-se na ingrata água da chuva.
Não sei se ao escrever este poema
Quebrarei as grilhetas das gotas da chuva

Não sei, não sei
Se escrever este poema é o ideal
Enquanto lá fora a água ama a terra
E a chuva continua arquitectando o seu poema
E cá, na minha frente
Impiedosamente a chama da vela
Lambe o saturado ar do meu quarto

Não sei se é justo
A minha pena de cabeceira
Beijar o pergaminho
Neste solene e sagrado momento
Em que a água calidamente
Se perde nas entranhas da terra
E que o corpo da vela
Paulatinamente se derrete

Coroado com a sua impiedosa chama. . .
Não, não sei
Vou parar, mas. . . Não sei. . .

> Sal Island, September 1980
> *Aulil.* Ilha do Sal, Município do Sal,
> 1987, pp. 93–94.

Indecision

> (For the Meteorologists, my colleagues)

I don't know, I don't know
If writing this poem is the right thing
While the rain is singing
Its songs on the rooftop and is stroking the ground

I don't know
If the hour is propitious
For plucking a poem
In the candle's dim light
While the current has failed

I don't know
Should I listen to the patter
Or write and follow its rhythm . . .
I awakened and thought I would write
On this rainy night in September . . .

I don't know
If by writing my unrhymed lines
I'll disrupt the dripping water . . .
The storm stopped the show in the movies
Its fury has cut the current
  (That's what I saw through the window)

I don't know . . . what am I to do . . .
Screams and booms I hear
Thunder and shouts of youngsters
Youngsters cleansing themselves in the troublesome rain . . .
I don't know if by writing these verses
I shall break the fetters of raindrops

I don't know, I don't know
If writing this poem is the right thing
While outside the water makes love to the earth
And the rain keeps composing its own lyric song
And here in the room while standing before me
The merciless candle
Is lapping my room's heavy air

I don't know if it's proper
For my pen on the bedstand
To be kissing the parchment
At such a solemn moment like this
When water from heaven so warmly
Is running off into earth's womb
And a body of beeswax
Is melting ever so slowly
Crowned by its merciless flame . . .
No, I don't know
I'll stop now, but wait . . . I don't know . . .

Jorge Tolentino

Brisas de ontem

1

— Vida de tchuco — ouvi papai gritar lá na pé-de-porta. Era sempre a mesma coisa. Levantava-se cedo, baixava para a Morada e quando as onze horas aprontavam-se, regressava mudo nem uma rocha, quando não vinha descompondo todo o mundo. Hoje ele estava alvoroçado.

Mamãe estava num canto a amamentar Picnitchim e levantou-se de um salto, deixando o bébé a berros e águas, quando ouviu papai chegar.

— Então, António? Toma com calma. Larga tudo nas mãos de Deus — dizia ela.

E papai exaltava-se mais: Não senhora! Isso não pode continuar!

— Nenhum filho-de-parida pode mudar mundo e destino de homem — profetizava a minha mãe.

— Qual destino! Destino é a gente morrer de fome se não aparece trabalho. E há muito trabalho para fazer. Por que é que não fazem Sãocente como naquele postal que o teu primo mandou de Holanda?

— Não é Holanda, papai, é França — interrompi-o.

— França, Holanda ou Lisboa não interessa, seu descarado.

Recebi caro pela ousadia.

E ele falava, falava, excitando-se cada vez mais. Que haveria trabalho, boniteza na rua, ninguém ouviria meninos a chorar de fome. . .

— E agora António? — intervinha mamãe. — O Governador não ouve ninguém.

Papai pareceu acalmar-se: — Ouve quem quer. Ouve quem tem casa e carro e não precisa de nada. Isto está para ricos — disse ele numa voz baixa e enérgica que não consegui entender.

Resolvi sair dali. Sentei-me atrás do portão e fiquei apanhando fresco. Daí a pouco abriam-no de repelão contra as minhas costas. Dei um pulo e só gritei ao aterrar.

Filipa riu-se do meu grito e disse: — Anda daí, seu lofa, vem ajudar-me.

— Larga-me da mão, sua não sabe bater.

Ela fingiu-se estafada e uivava: — Ah Mamãe, João não quer ajudar-me. Ui, ui, ui. . .

Olha a besta a berrar! . . .

Mamãe gritou-me: — João, ajuda a Filipa. Menino de não sei quem. Mas eu sei o que é que tu queres: é porrada.

Fui ajudá-la tremendo de raiva. Apeteceu-me dar-lhe um banho com a comida de tchuco. Era só dizer que tinha agarrado mal a lata. Não fossem os porcos. . . Eram capazes de embirrar comigo. Coitados. Se falassem, de certeza que saberiam pedir desculpas. Imaginei a cena e pus-me a rir com gosto. Nesta altura mamãe passava ao pé de mim e fez menção de me dar uma bofetada, enquanto dizia: — Devera, devera vocês de hoje em dia não tem consideração.

Via-a apanhar uma bolsa e sair. Devia ter ido à mercearia. Oxalá ela conseguisse fiado.

Aproximava-se a hora da escola. Lembrei-me de umas contas que tinha por fazer. Fui buscar a pasta e sentei-me num canto a fazê-las. 9 × 7 são 54, não, 59. . . não. Bolas, onde está a tabuada? Ah, hum. . . As contas cansavam-me a cabeça e a minha fome aumentava. Era a única conta que estava a dar certa.

À noitinha, quando as estrelas pontearam o céu e as luzes começaram a brilhar atrás do Porto-Grande, ferindo as águas tranquilas da baía, mamãe e papai saíram rumo à casa de Nha Joana d'Gustim, onde o candeeiro cintilava encharcando de uma luz vermelha as pessoas que aí se encontravam a tomar parte na dor de Nha Joana.

Apertava o coração vê-la chorar. Coitada. Coitado também do Tony. Quatro anos e já morto. Era uma graça de boize. Encontrava-me vê-lo a correr por aí, nu em pelôte, atirando pedras. Fazia-me rir quando subia em cima dos montes de cascalho de Nhô Griga e fazia serviço, rindo e saboreando antecipadamente as guerras do proprietário. E, quando via-o assomar com uma vara, escanelava-se carregando o seu corpo ossudo. Depois era o gozo de sempre: — Uá, lá, la ti Griga, uá la lá ti Griga.

Fui sentar-me na soleira da porta com o Zeca, Filipa e Picnitchim. A este fiz uma festa e o malandro pôs-se a chorar.

— Pensou que ias tirar-lhe a chucha-de-açúcar — explicou a Filipa. Todos os meninos estavam tristes e sonolentos. Não podiam fazer roda, nem cantar, e quem podia contar histórias estava na casa-de-morto.

Daí a pouco começou a soprar um ventinho fresco e Filipa entrou com o bébé. Dois cachorros passaram a correr atrás de um gato. Este guindou numa parede, fez-se corcunda e descompôs os perseguidores. Mas os senhores cachorros não arredavam os pés e latiam, latiam. . . Os malandros estavam sempre prontos para exibir a sua antiga amizade.

Zeca começou a remar. Senti-me cansado também. Lembrei-me que o enterro era no dia seguinte de manhã e resolvi entrar. Arrastei comigo o Zeca que, entretanto, arranhava já o primeiro sono.

2

Madrugada ainda verde e eu já acordado! ? . . . O que é que havia comigo? Onde estava a minha fama de dorminhoco? Eu tinha um estranho pressentimento que não me deixava dormir.

Papai ainda estava roncando. Mamãe já devia estar acordada a preparar o seu dia. Ouvi o porco grunhir. Lembrei-me do galo. A que hora cantaria ele? Nunca o tinha ouvido. O porco voltou a grunhir, desta vez com menos força. Grunhia, grunhia cada vez mais baixo e distante. Sim, era isso, ia-se distanciando. Correu-me ideia em ladrões. Nisto ouvi mamãe gritar:

— António, acorda. Estão a roubar o porco.

Pus-me a tremer e escondi-me de encontro à cama. Vi papai abrir a porta e sair, empunhando a sua catana. Mamãe riscou a cara com o Sinal da Cruz e fez-se ao largo com a tranca da porta nas mãos.

Zeca acordou e perguntou com voz espantada: — O que é, mamãe? Papai? Ninguém respondeu.

Eu tinha os olhos pesados. Senti frio e a tremura aumentou. Daí a pouco adormecia.

3

— Eh, John, John, levanta-te rapaz. — Era o Zeca a acordar-me. — Tu nunca ouves nada, senhor dorminhoco. Tens um sono pesado, hem! Como pedra. Esta madrugada iam roubando o nosso porco. Ó que barulho! . . . Moço! Aquilo, só visto: a vizinhança acordada, o porco correndo por um lado e o ladrão escapando por outro. . .

Resolvi interrompê-lo: — Conseguiam apanhar o porco?

— Qual?

— O nosso. O porco de verdade — respondi rindo.

— Ah, o nosso, sim, conseguimos — respondeu-me e prosseguiu; — Os cachorros latiam que era um consolo. Se o pirata não tivesse escanelado, ficava em tiras.

Saímos para fora. Mamãe tratava do porco.

— Bom dia, mamãe — cumprimentei.

— Bom dia, nha filho, dormiste bem?

— Sim. . . mamãe — murmurei.

— Já viste que nos queriam tirar o porco? — perguntou-me ela. — O mundo está cheio de gente má, braba mesmo. Não sei o que seria de nós. . . O tchuco enquanto está lá é uma certeza.

Papai chegou naquele momento e pedi-lhe que me botasse a bênção, ao que ele me respondeu: — Deus te abençoe e te dê um sono mais leve. Deves deixar o sono pesado só para as pedras. Um homem deve espantar o sono mal ouça qualquer barulhinho.

Bateram. Fui abrir o portão e Nha Armandinha entrou, ofegante, disparando logo: — Ah nhas gente, vocês contem lá como foi.

— Ah comadre Armandinha, você está vendo uma coisa? — fêz mamãe com as mãos atracadas à cintura.

Retirei-me deixando-as falar e a julgar as coisas deste planeta. Era só visto a atenção com que o porco escutava a conversa.

4

Aí pelas três horas, quando começámos a almoçar, fazia um sol quente. Eu ainda sentia-me cansado do percurso fúnebre. O sol torrou-nos, abusando da lentidão dos nossos passos. Lembrei-me dos turistas aprumados em cima dum camião, a fotografar-nos. Um deles tinha uma pança, tão redondinha que, ao vê-la, não pude deixar de acariciar a minha, murcha e desgostosa.

Resolvi abandonar as recordações: — Papai, por que é que a gente deita uma mão de terra na cova, sobre o caixão?

Aquilo é uma despedida — disse-me ele — quando o meu pai nasceu ele encontrou aquilo, eu encontrei, o meu avô também. Sempre existiu. É um hábito.

Mamãe interveio: — Devera, devera, uma pessoa não é nada neste mundo. Nasce-se pequeno e vai-se onde Deus quiser. Cada um tem o seu fim consoante o seu destino.

Eu e Filipa entreolhamo-nos e senti-me desgostoso. Tentei afastar a pergunta que me atormentava: seria doloroso morrer?

Houve um longo silêncio, apenas violado pelo zum-zum das moscas e pelos grunhidos do porco. Ele devia ter fome: um. . . um. . . um. . .

Papai cortou o silêncio: — Mari Júlia, . . . Meninos, eu tenho estado a pensar. . . — Fez uma pausa e continuou: — Decidi ir dar uma volta por este mundo fora.

— Credo, homem de Deus, o que é que tu tens na cabeça? — esconjurou mamãe.

Papai abanou a cabeça, fez um sorriso amargo e disse: — Eu não tenho nada, Mari Júlia. A gente tem que sair, procurar vida. Isto está cada vez mais difícil e os meninos estão a crescer. . . Um pai tem que mexer.

— Para onde é que voce vai, papai? — perguntou o Zeca.

— Não sei, filho. Vou andar. Lá fora encontro trabalho de certeza.

Mamãe discordava com tristeza: — Mas João, a gente vai aguentando. Sempre estamos na nossa terra.

— Não. Já não há que aguentar. A gente tem que abrir os olhos, senão acabamos morrendo todos de fome — disse o meu pai com voz decidida.

Filipa interveio: — Você vai já, papai?

— Ainda não sei. É preciso preparar, dar voltas. . . Fez-se silêncio. Papai perguntou-me se não dizia nada.

— Ficarei com saudades, papai — murmurei — mas eu acho que você deve ir devera.

— Anda cá rapaz — papai abraçou-me e tentou animar o ambiente:

— Então, nhas gente? O comandante vai mas o João fica a substituir.

Zeca riu às gargalhadas. Mamãe observou: — Cuidado não digas isso ao João. Bem sabes como é que ele é.

— Ahn — fez papai.

— Ele quererá governar-me — concluiu ela.

Papai pôs-se a rir enquanto Zeca e Filipa faziam-me biocos.

(Mindelo, October 1979)
Raízes, no. 21. Praia, June 1984,
Beginning of a tale, pp. 79–83.

Breezes of Yesteryear

1

"It's a porker's life, that's what it is," I heard Dad shout over there on the doorstep. It was always like that. He would get up early, go downtown and when it was getting close to eleven, he'd return without a word, more mute than a rock, or else he would cuss everybody. Today he was upset.

Mom had been in a corner, giving Itsybitsy her breast, and she got up with a start, letting the baby howl and wet itself, as soon as she had heard Dad come.

"Well, Antonio? Take it easy. Leave it in God's hands," she said.

And Dad would get more upset: "No, no, no, woman. Things can't go on like that!"

"Man born of woman can't change the world and his fate," augured my mother.

"Fate? What do you mean? Is that fate that people are starving to death if no one gives them work? And there's plenty of work to be done. Why don't they make Sãocente Island like what's on that postcard that your cousin sent from Holland?"

"Not Holland, Dad, France," I chimed in.

"France, Holland, Lisbon, what does it matter, you brat."

I paid dearly for my arrogance.

And he talked on and on, getting more and more excited. There would be enough work, the streets would look nice, nobody would hear children crying because they were hungry . . .

"And what can be done now, Antonio?" Mom intervened. "The Governor won't listen to anybody."

Dad seemed to calm down: "He listens to whom he wants. He listens to those who have a house and a car and don't need anything. This system is for the rich," said he in a low, determined voice. I could not hear what followed.

I decided to go outside. I sat down behind the gate and caught a whiff of the cool breeze. Shortly the gate was pushed open against my back. I gave a jump and screamed as soon as I hit the ground.

My scream made Philippa laugh, and she said: "Get going, you bum, come and help me."

"Take your hand off of me, your hand is too weak to beat."

She pretended to be tired and howled: "Heh, Mom, John refuses to help me. Ah me, ah me, ah me . . ."

"Just look at that cow mooing! . . ."

Mom shouted at me: "John, you help Philippa. I don't know whom that boy takes after. But I know what you need: a good licking."

Trembling with anger, I went and helped her. I felt like dowsing her with the porker's slop. All she had to say was that I wasn't holding the pail right. If it weren't for the pigs . . . They might take it out on me. Poor things. If they could talk surely they'd beg me to forgive them. I pictured the droll scene and burst out laughing. At that point Mom passed by me and threatened to slap me, saying: "Really, really, youngsters show no consideration nowadays."

I saw her pick up a shopping bag and leave. She must have gone to the grocery. Let's hope they let her buy on credit.

It was getting to be time for school. I remembered I still had to do some math problems. I looked for my satchel and sat down in a corner to do them. 9 × 7, 54, no, 59 . . . no. Nuts! Where's my multiplication table?

ah, hm . . . Problems tired my brain and made me grow hungrier. That was the only problem for which I knew the solution.

At nightfall, when the stars dotted the sky and the lights began to blink behind the Big Harbor, striking the calm waters of the bay, Mom and Dad headed for the house of 'Gustin's Miz Johanna, where the lantern sparkled, casting a reddish light on the persons gathered there to share Miz Johanna's grief.

It broke one's heart to see her weep. Poor woman. And poor Tony. Only four years old and dead already. He had been such a cute little bozo. I still could see him running around stark naked and throwing stones. He used to make me laugh as he climbed up on Mr. Griga's gravel mounds to relieve himself there, grinning in anticipation of the owner's fits. And when he saw him appear with a stick, he took to his heels stretching his skinny body. After that he would hoot at the man: "hulloh, hulloh, hulloh, nuncle Griga! Hulloh, hulloh, hulloh, nuncle Griga!"

I went and sat down on the doorstep beside Joey, Philippa and Itsybitsy. I petted him and the little bugger started to cry.

"He thought you were taking his pacifier away," Philippa explained.

All of the children were moping and getting sleepy. They couldn't form a circle or sing, and the grownups who could have told stories were at the dead urchin's house.

Shortly thereafter, a cool breeze began to blow, and Philippa went back into the house with the baby. Two curs raced by in pursuit of a cat. The cat jumped upon a wall, arched its back and hissed at its pursuers. But their honors, the curs, did not run off; they barked and barked . . . The scoundrels were always eager to show off their ancient affinity with cats.

Joey began to fight against sleep. I, too, felt tired. It occurred to me that the burial would be in the morning and so I made up my mind to go in. I dragged Joey with me, who was already half asleep.

2

The dawn was still young and I already awake? ! . . . What was wrong with me? Wasn't I known as a sleepyhead? I had a strange foreboding, which did not let me sleep.

Dad was still snoring. Mom must have been awake already making preparations for her day. I heard the pig grunt. I thought of the rooster. When would he crow? I'd never heard him. The pig grunted again, less loudly this time. Its grunt sounded lower each time and more distant. That was it, it was moving away. The thought of thieves crossed my mind. At that moment, I heard Mom scream:

"Antonio, wake up. They're stealing the pig!"

I began to tremble and hid against the bed. I saw Dad open the door and leave, clutching his machete. Mom crossed herself and sailed out with the crossbar of the door in her hands.

Joey woke up and asked with fear in his voice:

"What is it, Mom? Dad?" No one answered.

My eyes felt heavy. I was cold and shivered more and more violently. Shortly I fell asleep.

3

"Heh, John, John, get up, you guy." It was Joey, waking me up. "You never hear a thing, Mister Sleepyhead. You're a deep sleeper, eh! Like a log. Today at dawn they were about to steal our pig. Oh, what a racket! . . . Man! You should have seen it: the whole neighborhood awake, the pig running in one direction, the thief escaping in another . . ."

I had to interrupt him. "Did they catch the pig?"

"Which?"

"Ours. The actual pig," I replied, laughing.

"Oh yes, ours, we did," he answered and continued: "The dogs were barking: it was a joy to hear them. If the gangster hadn't taken to his heels they would have torn him to pieces."

We went outside. Mom was taking care of the pig.

"Good morning, Mom," I greeted her.

"Good morning, Sonny, did you sleep well?"

"Yes'm," I mumbled.

"Can you imagine, they tried to rob our pig?" she asked me. "The world is full of bad people, brutes even. I don't know what would have become of us. As long as the porker is there we are sure of something."

Dad arrived at that moment, and I asked him for his blessing. His response was: "May God bless you and give you sleep that's less profound. Leave deep sleep to the logs. A man should banish sleep when he hears the slightest noise."

Someone knocked. I went to open the gate, and Miz Armandinha entered out of breath and at once fired away: "Oh, my dears, tell me how it happened."

"Oh, my good Armandinha, have you ever seen a thing like this?" Mom said, with her arms akimbo.

I withdrew, letting them talk and opine about the things on this planet Earth. You should have seen how attentively the pig was listening to the conversation.

4

About three in the afternoon, when we were starting our lunch, the sun was beating down fiercely. I was still worn out from walking in the funeral procession. The sun had toasted us, taking an unfair advantage of our slow march. I recalled tourists standing up on a truck to take our pictures. One of them had such a perfectly round belly, I couldn't help stroking my own wrinkled and sad stomach at the sight of it.

I dismissed those recollections. "Dad, what's the reason people throw a handful of earth on the coffin in the grave?"

"That's a way of leave taking," said he. "When my father was born it already was that way, it was that way when I was born, and also when my grandfather was. It has always existed. It's a custom."

Mom chimed in: "Really, really, a body is nothing in this world. One is born a little tot, and one goes to where God wants one to. Each has the end that's destined for him."

Philippa and I exchanged looks, and I felt dissatisfied. I tried to put off the question that troubled me: Would death be painful?

There was a long silence, barely broken by the buzzing of flies and the grunts of the pig. The pig must have been hungry: "Oink . . . oink . . . oink . . ."

Dad broke the silence: "Marijulia . . . Children, I have been thinking . . . He paused, then continued: "I've decided to take a little tour through the world outside."

"Goodness gracious, man, what's gotten into your head?" Mom lamented.

Dad nodded, cracked a bitter smile and said: "Nothing wrong with me, Marijulia. A body has to get out and look for a way to make a living. Here conditions are becoming tougher all the time, and the children are growing up . . . A father has to bestir himself."

"Where are you going, Dad?" our Joey asked.

"I don't know, son. I'll be on the move. Out there I'm sure I'll find work."

Full of sorrow, Mom disagreed: "But John, we'll manage. At least, here we're in our own country."

"No. There's no way to manage any longer. We have got to open our eyes, or else we'll all starve to death in the end," my father said with a voice of one who's made up his mind.

Philippa chimed in: "You leave right away, Dad?"

"I don't know yet. There are preparations to be made, steps to be taken . . ." Silence. Dad asked me if I had nothing to say.

"I'll miss you, Dad," I mumbled. "But I think you definitely should go."

"Come here, boy," and Dad put his arms around me and tried to dispel the gloom:

"Well now, folks? The captain goes but our John stays here to take his place."

Joey laughed and laughed. Mom remarked: "You better don't tell John such things. You know full well what he's like."

"Mmmm," Dad replied.

"He'll want to boss me," was her conclusion.

Dad started to laugh while Joey and Philippa made faces at me.

APPENDIX B:
CAPE VERDEAN CHRONOLOGY, 1974–1991

Year	General Events	New Publications of Older Writers	Periodicals
1974	(April) De-facto decolonization		*Terra Nova* (April), São Filipe, ed. "Antalgo" (António Fidalgo Barros)
			Ariópe (June), Praia, ed. Oswaldo Osório
1975	(July 5) Political independence granted		
1976	Creation of the *Instituto Caboverdiano do Livro*, Praia		
1977	A writers' delegation headed by A.A. Gonçalves met with Senegalese writers in Dakar		*Raízes* (Jan./April), Praia, ed. Arnaldo França
1981	*Canto liberto*, anthology of poems by 12 young people, prefaced by A.A. Gonçalves, pub. by JAAC-CV, Praia		*Folhas Verdes*, Praia, ed. Arménio Vieira *Despertar*, Praia, ed. students of the Liceu Ludgero Lima
1982	*Contravento*, Taunton, Mass., anthology of poetry, ed. Luís Romano		
1983			*Ponto & Vírgula* (February/March), Mindelo, ed. Germano Almeida, Leão Lopes and Rui Figueiredo

Year	General Events	New Publications of Older Writers	Periodicals
1985	Revised ed. of *A aventura crioula*, a history of Cape Verdean literature by Manuel Ferreira, Lisbon	*Noite de vento*, Praia, collected stories by A.A. Gonçalves	*Arquipélago* (May), Boston, Mass., ed. Virgínio de Melo ("Teobaldo Virgínio")
1986	Creation of a *Ministério da Cultura*, Praia	*Cântico da manhã futura*, Praia, collected poems by "Osvaldo Alcântara" (Baltasar Lopes)	*Seiva* (November), Praia, organ of JAAC-CV, ed. Arnaldo Andrade, Emanuel Brito, Alexandre S. Semedo, Manuel B. Semedo, Adla Regala
	Symposium in Mindelo to commemorate 50th anniversary of *Claridade*		
(1986)	Founding of the *Pró-Cultura* Movement, Praia, by young writers and artists		*Voz di Letra* (March) Praia, ed. Ondina Ferreira and Oswaldo Osório. *Sopinha do Alfabeto*, (November), Praia
1987	*Mornas para piano*, Mindelo, Cape Verdean dance tunes and songs, ed. "Jôtamont" (Jorge Fernandes Monteiro)	*Os trabalhos e os dias*, Lisbon, collected stories by Baltasar Lopes	*Aurora*, Praia (2 issues), ed. students of the Liceu Domingos Ramos
	Na bóka noti, Collected folk tales, ed. T.V. da Silva		*Fragmentos* (August), Praia, organ of the *Pró-Cultura* Movement, ed. José Luís Hopffer C. Almada
	Oju d'águ, first novel written in Santiago Crioulo, by Manuel Veiga, Praia		
1988	*56 mornas de Cabo Verde*, Mindelo, collected by "Jôtamont" (Jorge Fernandes Monteiro)		*Magma*, (April), São Filipe, ed. Arnaldo Silva
	Across the Atlantic, North Dartmouth, Mass., anthology of poetry and prose in English trans., ed. Maria M. Ellen		

Year	General Events	New Publications of Older Writers	Periodicals
1989	Creation of the Association of Cape Verdean Writers	*O escravo*, Lisbon, reedition of the first Cape Verdean novel (1856), by José Evaristo d'Almeida, a Portuguese settler	*Djâr d'Sal*, Sal Island
		Poesias, I, Praia, collected poems by Jorge Barbosa	
1991	(January 13) The single-party regime that had ruled since 1975 was voted out of power		*Artiletra*, Mindelo
	Mirabilis, Lisbon, Anthology of the latest generation of Cape Verdean poets, ed. J. L. Hopffer Almada		

APPENDIX C: BIBLIOGRAPHY

NB. Some Abbreviations

(E)	literary essay	(P)	poem(s)
ed.	edited by, editor(s)	pr.pr.	privately printed
ib.	ibidem, in the same	(PS)	prose sketch
	periodical	(S)	story, stories
ICL	Instituto Caboverdiano	(T)	theater
	do Livro		
(N)	novel		

Works by the Nine Writers Singled Out in This Study

Two Precursors

ARMÉNIO VIEIRA (born on Santiago Island, 1941)

"Não sei o que daria," *Cabo Verde* (Praia), no. 137(1961), p. 14.   (P)
"Contenção e renúncia," ib., no. 153(1961), p. 36.   (P)
"Mar! Mar! . . .," *Sèló* (Mindelo), no. 2(1962).   (P)
"Talvez un dia. . .," *Mákua*, vol. I, pp. 21–25. Sá da Bandeira, (Angola),   (P)
     Imbondeiro, 1962.
"Evocação da minha infância," "Vai e diz!" ib.   (P)
"Isto é o que fazem de nós!," *Vértice* (Coimbra), nos. 334/335(1971).   (P)
"Toti Cadabra," ib.   (P)
"Com letras de revolta," "Canto do futuro," *Ariópe* (Praia), no. 1(1974),   (P)
     pp. 3, 4.
"Como deuses debaixo do sol," ib., no. 2(1974), p. 4   (P)
"Para uma vida plena de consciência da terra," ib., no. 4(1974), p. 3   (P)
"Desmistificação de Pasárgada," "Kanta ku alma sem ser magoado," ib.   (P)
"Descrição de um pesadelo," *Raízes* (Praia), no. 2(1977), pp. 73–76.   (S)
Cabo Verde. Praia, Editorial CIDAC, 1979.   (P)
"Helena mirha cabra," "Não há estátua que preste na minha cidade,"   (P)
     Raízes (Praia), nos. 17/20(1981), pp. 101–104.
Poemas 1971–1979. Lisbon, África Editora, 1981.   (P)
"Dou-te sempre um cigarro," *Ponto & Vírgula* (Mindelo), no. 5(1983), p. 33.   (S)
"Tó qui noti bira dia," "Kanta ku alma sem ser magoado," "Nôs bandera,"   (P)
     in Luís Romano, ed., *Contravento*. Taunton, Mass., 1982, pp. 46–51,
     with translations into standard Portuguese.
"As coisas deste mundo e do outro," *Ponto & Vírgula* (Mindelo), no. 8   (S)
     (1984), p. 26.
"Fumando charutos velhos e caríssimos," *Voz di Letra* (Praia), no. 4(1986), p. 8.   (S)
"Prenda de Natal," *Fragmentos* (Praia), no. 1(1987), p 8.   (S)
"O assassino," ib., nos. 3/4(1988), p. 14.   (S)

"Our flag," English translation of "Nôs bandera," and "Poem," English   (P)
translation of "Mar! Mar!," in M.M. Ellen, ed., *Across the Atlantic*.
N. Dartmouth, Mass., 1988, pp. 23, 43.

O eleito do sol. Lisbon, 1989.   (N)

"Eu—de repente," "Poema final," "Never more," "Nenhum rio é grande   (P)
demais," *Fragmentos*, nos. 5/6(1989), p. 77.

"Duela de fogo," "Amo-te," "Fala o papa João Paulo Segundo," "Se eu   (P)
tivesse instrumentos cortantes," ib., nos. 7/8(1991), p. 26.

CORSINO FORTES (born in Mindelo, 1933)

"Mindelo," *Boletim dos Alunos do Liceu Gil Eanes* (Mindelo), no. 1(1959).   (P)

"Girassol," "Vendeta" "Pecado original," "Meio-dia," "Paixão," "Noite de   (P)
S. Silvestre," *Claridade* (Mindelo), no. 9(1960), pp. 24–30.

"Ode para além do choro," *Cabo Verde* (Praia), no. 138(1961).   (P)

Pão & fonema. Lisbon, Sá da Costa, 1974.   (P)

"Tchon de pove tchon de pedra," "Pesadèle na terra de gente ou pesadèle   (P)
em trânsito," "Konde palmanhã manché," "Tchuva," in Luís Romano,
ed., *Contravento*. Taunton, MA, 1982, pp. 64–77, with translations into
standard Portuguese.

Árvore & tambor. Praia, ICL, 1986.   (P)

"Rain," English translation of "Tchuva," and "Emigrant," English translation   (P)
of "Emigrante," in M.M. Ellen, ed., *Across the Atlantic*. N. Dartmouth,
Mass., 1988, pp. 35, 53ff.

Seven Members of the Independence Generation

JOSÉ LUÍS HOPFFER C. ALMADA ("Dionísio de Deus y Fontana," "Alma
Dofer," "Zé di Sant'y Agu," "Erasmo Cabral d'Almada"; born on
Santiago Island, 1965)

"Memória para Jorge Barbosa," *Voz di Letra* (Praia), no. 1(1986), p. 3.   (P)

"Verde afã ou uma palavra vã," ib., no. 3(1986), p. 1.   (P)

"Permanência," ib., no. 4(1986), p. 4.   (P)

"País ilhéu," ib., no. 5(1986), p. 6.   (P)

"Meio-dia putrefacto," *Seiva* (Praia), no. 5(1987), p. 25.   (P)

"Exercício poético sobre a cor e o amor," "Para Vadinho, o possesso da   (P)
eternidade," *Fragmentos* (Praia), no. 1(1987), pp. 15, 39.

"O convívio. . .," ib., pp. 5–6.   (S)

"Margo," ib., no. 2(1988), pp. 15–17.   (PS)

"Angústia," ib., no. 2(1988), p. 27.   (P)

"Ta madura na spiga," "Buska," "Poema ante o crepúsculo," ib., nos.   (P)
3/4(1988), pp. 44, 49.

"Depoimento in memoriam de Baltazar Lopes," ib., nos. 5/6(1989), pp. 9–10.   (E)

"*O julgamento* de Ano Novo," ib., nos. 5/6(1989), p. 30.   (E)

"Fede o féretro," "Exílio," "In memoriam de Che Guevara," "Cicatrizes da   (P)
seca," "Brain storming," ib., nos. 5/6(1989), pp. 47–48.

"Rememoração da terra e da humidade," ib., nos. 5/6(1989), pp. 63–64.   (S)

"Lenbransas di arvi," ib., nos. 5/6(1989), pp. 71–72.   (PS)

"Chuva nocturna," ib., nos. 5/6(1989), pp. 79–80.   (S)

"Na morte de Osvaldo Alcântara (versão primeira)," ib., nos. 5/6(1989),   (P)
pp. 93–94.

"Tudo se suicida na poesia!" "Naufrágio," "Modorra," "Rijinerason: Es (P)
toma nu rostu . . .; A pedra e a ribeira; Não tem relógios . . .,"
Fragmentos, nos. 7/8(1991), p. 27f.

ALBERTO FERREIRA GOMES ("Binga"; born in Mindelo, 1957)

"Tamarindeiro mártir," *Terra Nova* (Mindelo), no. 59(1980), p. 2. (P)
"Convite," ib., no. 62(1980), p. 6. (P)
"Fogo-festa," ib., no. 65(1980), p. 6. (P)
"Canção do vento," ib., no. 66(1980), p. 4. (P)
"Doutor Calú d'Antoninha," ib., no. 70(1981), p. 6. (S)
"Eu também a procuro," ib., no. 82(1982), p. 4. (P)
"Uma criança desolada," *Ponto & Vírgula* (Mindelo), no. 9(1984), (S)
pp. 25–26.
"A trilha," *Fragmentos* (Praia), no. 1(1987), pp. 11–13. (S)
"Três vectores—uma resultante," "Tamarindeiro mártir," "Navegações," (P)
"Peregrins d'paz," "Presságio," "Enterro do poeta," "Insaciável,"
"Indecisão," "Suplício," and "Alucinações," in *Aulil*. Sal Island,
Município, 1987, pp. 10, 18–19, 36–37, 42–43, 53–54, 61–63, 79–80,
93–94, 103–104, 110.
"A trilha," ib., pp. 45–50. (S)
"Vestes de poeta," *Fragmentos* (Praia), no. 3/4(1988), p. 41. (P)

TOMÉ VARELA DA SILVA (born on Santiago Island, 1950)

Finasons di ña Nasia Gomi, ed. Praia, ICL, 1985. (E)
Kumuñon d'África: Onti, oŝi, mañan. Praia, ICL, 1986. (P)
Kardisantus. Praia, ICL, 1987. (P)
Na bóka noti, vol. I, ed. with A. Semedo. Praia, ICL, 1987. (E, PS)
Natal y kontus. Praia, ICL, 1988. (S)
Ña Bibiña Kabral, ed. with H. Santos and A. Semedo. Praia, ICL, 1988. (E)
Escada de luz. Praia, ICL, 1989. (P)
Ña Gida Mendi: Simenti di onti na ĉon di mañan, ed. Praia, ICL, 1990. (E)

ALEXANDRE S. SEMEDO ("Alsasem"; born on Santiago Island, 1956)

"Mangui—cidadi di manham," *Terra Nova* (Mindelo), no. 71(1981), p. 5. (PS)
"O luminári de São João nos Órgãos," ib., no. 85(1982), p. 3. (PS)
"Konkista," ib., no. 100(1984), p. 4. (P)
"Bibinha Cabral: mulher, mãe e artista," *Voz di Letra* (Praia), no. 4(1986), (E)
p. 6.
"Banalidade," *Seiva* (Praia), no. 5(1987), p. 23. (P)

JORGE CARLOS FONSECA ("José Fonseca Duarte"; born in Mindelo,
São Vicente Island, 1950)

"A (não) gramática da poesia," "A matemática da liberdade," "Conjugação (P)
nocturna," "Poema da amanhã," *Raízes* (Praia), no. 1(1977), pp. 84–87.
"Eu nunca diria tenho medo ou não tenho medo da morte," "Polivitamina (P)
de meus sonhos," "O simulacro do suicídio," ib., no. 2(1977),
pp. 84–86.
"Beija-me, palavra," "Eu cá não temo as palavras," ib., no. 3(1977), pp. 66–69. (P)
"Mar e sal para os crustáceos," "E porque não a poesia?," ib., nos. 5/6(1978), (P)
pp. 112–113.

"Saxofone de espuma," "Poema de amanhã," "Ferro & alumínio & cimentos   (P)
     & pozolana & chuva se vier," "Poema do destemor," "Poesiaaa,
     ombrooo armaaas," "Para ti amor-sem-dicionários," in *Jogos Florais*
     12 de Setembro 1976. Praia, ICL, n.d. (1978?), pp. 35–48.
"Morremos todos os dias na América," "Quis-te ausente, poesia   (P)
     interdita. . ." *África* (Lisbon), no. 4(1979), pp. 427–431.
"Homofonias da aritmética," *Voz di Letra* (Praia), no. 5(1986), p. 8.   (P)
"Quatro tempos-o-mesmo-vento," *Fragmentos* (Praia), no. 1(1987), p. 30.   (P)
"A morte viva do silêncio," ib., no. 2(1988), p. 52.   (P)
"Não nos respondam. . .," ib., no. 5/6(1989), p. 58.   (P)

Jorge Tolentino ("Moninfeudo"; born in Mindelo, 1963)

"A chefe," *África* (Lisbon), no. 9(1980), pp. 481–484.   (S)
"Brisas de ontem," *Raízes* (Praia), no. 21(1984), pp. 79–107.   (S)
"A carta," *Ponto & Vírgula* (Mindelo), no. 15(1985), pp. 28–30.   (S)
(The first act of an untitled verse drama), *Fragmentos* (Praia), no. 1(1987),   (T)
     pp. 33–34.
"Natureza efémera," "Natureza viva," "Natureza agreste," "Natureza   (P)
     morta," ib., nos. 7/8(1991), p. 41.

Adelina C. da Silva (born in São Filipe, Fogo Island, ca. 1950)

"Macio como seda. . .," "Vida vazia," *Arquipélago* (Boston), no. 2(1985)   (P)
     p. 11.
"Busca," "Irmão," ib., no. 3(1986), p. 17.   (P)
"Fogo brando," "Mar," "Minha terra." "Retrato," ib., no. 5(1986),   (P)
     pp. xxv–xxvii.
"Mariposa," "Quotidiano," "O povo gritou há muito. . .," "No silêncio dos   (P)
     teus gestos. . .," ib., no. 7(1987), pp. 21–22.
"Amigo," "Confissão," ib., no. 8(1987), p. 17.   (P)
"Meu canto," "Regresso à terra," Nas águas do Charles," ib., no. 9(1988),   (P)
     pp. 36–37.
"Brother," "Saudades," "Quest," ib., no. 12(1989), pp. 28–29.   (P)
"Outro canto de liberdade," "O meu amor," "Tardes de sol," ib.,   (P)
     no. 14(1990), p. 31.
"Porque quando olhas para mim. . .?" "O meu jardim," ib., no. 15(1991),   (P)
     p. 18.
"Dia de São Valentim," "Sol di Jarfogo," "Desperdício," ib., no. 16(1991),   (P)
     p. 38.

Works by Twelve Other Writers of the Independence Generation

Vera Duarte (born in Mindelo, 1952)

"Na essência das coisas. . .," "A minha mão. . .," "Quis agarrar a noite   (P)
     com as mãos," "Dos rostos exangues. . .," "INDEPENDENTE!" "Não
     mais estradas percorridas. . .," A chuva caíu longamente. . .," in
     Jogos florais 12 de Setembro 1976. Praia, ICL, n.d. (1978?), pp. 57–70.
"Queria ser um poema lindo. . . ," *Raízes* (Praia), nos. 17/20(1981),   (P)
     pp. 108–110.
"Exercício poético 5," *Ponto & Vírgula* (Mindelo), no. 2(1983), p. 31.   (P)
"Exercício poético 7," ib., no. 3(1983), p. 35.   (P)

"Exercício poético 4," ib., no. 4(1983), p. 41.   (P)
"Exercícios poéticos 2, 8," *Raízes* (Praia), no. 21(1984), pp. 115–116.   (P)
"Corpo," *Fragmentos* (Praia), no. 1(1987), p. 17.   (P)
"O que tua boca calou. . .," ib., no. 2(1988), p. 13.   (P)
"Terra longe," "Não quero mals tornar. . .," ib., nos. 3/4(1988), p. 39.   (P)
"Rain," English translation, in M.M. Ellen, ed., *Across the Atlantic.*   (P)
    N. Dartmouth, Mass., 1988, p. 36.
"Adeus," "Ao fim. . .," "Carência," "Eu queria," ib., nos. 5/6(1989), p. 66.   (P)
"Querer," "E adorei-te," "Desejo," "Chuva," "Amigo," "Terra longe,"   (P)
    Fragmentos, nos. 7/8(1991), p. 42f.

JACQUES JAEL (born ca. 1950)

"Para quê qualquer poesia. . .," *Terra Nova* (Mindelo), no. 76(1981), p. 6.   (P)
"Distância," "Guentis antigu ta conta," ib., no. 82(1982), p. 5.   (P)
"Jorge Barbosa," "1982," ib., no. 89(1982), p. 4.   (P)
"Pa Silvenius," *Ponto & Vírgula* (Mindelo), no. 7(1984), p. 17.   (P)
"Noti," ib., no. 9(1984), p. 28.   (P)
"Di alto dum janela," ib., nos. 10/11(1984), p. 47.   (P)
"Sodaçan em letra grandi," *Terra Nova* (Mindelo), no. 117(1985), p. 4.   (P)

JOSÉ VICENTE LOPES ("Flávio Camilo"; born in Mindelo, São Vicente
    Island, 1959)

"A derrocada," *Ponto & Vírgula* (Mindelo), no. 6(1983), pp. 34–36.   (S)
"Novas estruturas poéticas e temáticas da poesia caboverdiana," ib.,   (E)
    no. 16(1986), pp. 19–23.
"Claridade, vanguarda, modernidade," *Terra Nova* (Mindelo),   (E)
    no. 128(1986), pp. 4, 6.
"A poética impoluta de [Osvaldo] Alcântara," ib., no. 136(1987), p. 4.   (E)
"Intelectual e intelectuais," *Fragmentos*, nos. 3/4(1988), pp. 76–81.   (E)
"Totens," "Gonçalviana," "O eixo e a roda," "Inscrição," "Requiem,"   (P)
    "Forever," "Guerra e Paz," "Anjos," "Solar," "Na terra," ib.,
    nos. 5/6(1989), p. 68.
"Escritura," "Retórica," "Calendário," "Cuidar dos vivos," "Epigrama,"   (P)
    "Ausência," "Plenitude," "Elegia de setembro," "Claridade," "Noutra
    terra," ib., nos. 7/8(1991), p. 47.

PAULA MARTINS ("Paula"; born on Santiago Island, 1957)

"Viva o M.P.L.A.!" *Voz di Povo* (Praia), September 4, 1975.   (P)
"Durante," "Para uma noite," "Desta manhã," *Raízes* (Praia), nos. 5/6(1978), (P)
    pp. 118–120.
"Saudação," "Vieste," ib., nos. 7/16(1980), pp. 119–121.   (P)
"Segredos por partilhar," "Mensagem – de Santa Cruz para minha Mãe,"   (P)
    Arquipélago (Boston), no. 13(1990), p. 20.
"Ilusão," ib., no. 1(1990), p. 33.   (P)
"Quisera . . ." ib., no. 15(1991), p. 21.   (P)

VASCO MARTINS (born in Queluz, Portugal, 1956)

Universo da ilha. Praia, ICL, 1986.   (P)
Diálogo poético sobre a música. Praia, ICL, n.d. (1987)   (E)

"A vida é uma quase planície," *Fragmentos* (Praia), no. 1(1987), p. 50.   (P)
"Poética musical," ib., no. 2(1988), pp. 53–54.   (PS)
Navegam os olhares com o vôo dos pássaros. Praia, ICL, 1989.   (P)
A música tradicional cabo-verdiana—I (A morna). Praia, ICLD, 1989.   (E)
A verdadeira dimensão. Linda-a-Velha (Portugal), ALAC, 1990.   (N)

FERNANDO MONTEIRO ("Jorge Andrade"; born ca. 1950)

"O crime da Praia Morena," *Fragmentos* (Praia), no. 1(1987), pp. 19–22.   (S)
"Desassossego, I," ib., no. 2(1988), pp. 21–23.   (S)
"Desassossego, II," ib., nos. 3/4(1988), pp. 15–18.   (S)
"A tragédia da Baía do Santo Nome," ib., nos. 5/6(1989), pp. 51–55.   (S)
"A máscara," "Chuva de outono," "A cerveja," "O órfão," "Uma rosa   (PS)
    negra para o meu irmão branco," ib., nos. 7/8(1991), pp. 75–77.

FLÁVIO MOREIRA ("Maria José"; born ca. 1950)

Quem é quem. Praia, ICL, 1988.   (T)

HUGO DUARTE FONSECA RODRIGUES (born on Fogo Island, ca. 1950)

"Dispertá," *Ariópe* (Praia), no. 4(1974), p. 4.   (P)
Burcan. São Filipe(?), pr.pr., 1974.   (S)
"Quem roubou a minha porta?" *Voz di Letra* (Praia), no. 4(1986), p. 2.   (S)
"Aeroporto," "Instantes," "Vida," "No alto," "Meu semelhante," "A frase,"   (P)
    "Momentos," "Serena," "Desespero," in *Aulil*, pp. 9, 26, 34–35, 41, 52,
    60, 90, 102, 109. Sal Island, Município, 1987.
"Marilha ou ilhamar," ib., pp. 28–30.   (S)
"Tchondicafé," *Magma* (São Filipe), no. 1(1988), pp. 16–17.   (S)

VALDEMAR VELHINHO RODRIGUES (born on Santiago Island, ca. 1950)

"Monólogos com (Calheta,) a minha aldeia: Pequena baía do meu   (P)
    coração. . .," "A casa da minha infância. . .," *Fragmentos* (Praia),
    no. 1(1987), p. 9.
"História verdadeira da Eva," ib., p. 9.   (P)
"Relâmpagos em terra: 3. Poema da última purificação; 9. Descoberta do   (P)
    Natal," ib., p. 9.
"À diferença," "Versos somente: À eternidade de Fernando Pessoa," ib.,   (P)
    p. 10.
"Apanhado surreal," *Fragmentos*, no. 2(1988), p. 26.   (P)
"Alguns dos meus poemas concretos?," ib., p. 34.   (P)
"Fragmentos: 4. O poeta quando está sentado"; 11. Debaixo do Sísifo,"   (P)
    Fragmentos, nos. 3/4(1988), p. 50.
"Quando em Deus penso e creio," "A imensa bondade dos fartos corvos,"   (P)
    "Interstício breve," "Dois," "Tristeza," "É bem natural," ib.,
    nos. 5/6(1989), pp. 44–46.
"Tenho no quarto as quatro estações . . .," "Quem-me-dera-quem-estar   (P)
    morto?" "Os outros do mundo vão indo," "xxxi–Ápice súbito,"
    "xiv–É a tarde," "xv–Consciência," "Insular," "Insularidade,"
    "Recantos," "Só," "Solidão," "Pássaros," "Grilos," "Paz," "Sonhos,"
    "Firmamento," ib., nos. 7/8(1991), pp. 48–53.

MADALENA TAVARES ("Lara Araújo"; born on Sal Island, 1951)

"Ilha do Sal," "Folha caída," "Vidas e palavras," "J mais A mais B,"   (P)
   "Canto 1," "Inspiração," "Ausência," "Santa Maria," "Amanhecer
   diferente," "Vida e agonia," in Aulil, pp. 11–12, 20, 27, 44, 55–56,
   64–65, 82, 85, 105, 111–112. Sal Island, Município, 1987.
"Emigrantes," ib., pp. 67–75.   (C)
"Momento," Fragmentos (Praia), no. 2(1988), p. 19.   (P)

FRANCISCO TOMAR ("Sukrato," "Sukre d'Sal," "João Tavares"; born on
   Boavista Island, 1951)

"Nilita," "Batuque," Morabeza (Rio de Janeiro), no. 5(1973), pp. 8, 13.   (P)
"Confissão," Presença Crioula (Lisbon), nos. 8/9(1973), p. 6.   (P)
"Amdjer preta," Morabeza (Rio de Janeiro), no. 6(1974), p. 6.   (P)
"Porque seria," "Festa de longe," ib., no. 7(1974), pp. 8, 14.   (P)
"Sonhe pa nha terra," ib., no. 9(1974), p. 4.   (P)
"Liberdade," "Mãe," ib., no. 11(1974), pp. 6, 7.   (P)
"Morabeza," ib., no. 12(1975), p. 8.   (P)
"Não me lavem o rosto," "Recordação," "Inquietação," in No reino de   (P)
   Caliban, vol. I, ed. Manuel Ferreira, pp. 255–256. Lisbon, Seara Nova,
   1975.
"Na grande hora," Nô Pintcha (Bissau), 1975.   (P)
"África," "Alvorada," Morabeza (Rio de Janeiro), no. 13(1976), pp. 16, 17.   (P)
Amdjers. Mindelo, pr.pr., 1977.   (P)
Horizonte aberto. Lisbon, Via Editora, n.d. (1977?).   (P)
"Ambiente: Djar d'Sal," "Identificaçon," in Contravento, ed. Luís Romano.   (P)
   Taunton, Mass., Atlantic Publishers, 1982, pp. 128–131, with translations
   into standard Portuguese.
"Sonhe pa nha terra," "Ambiente," "Identificaçon," in Luís Romano, ed.,   (P)
   Contravento. Taunton, Mass., Atlantic Publishers, 1982, pp. 126–131,
   with translations into standard Portuguese.
"Crepúsculo que não viu aurora," Ponto & Vírgula (Mindelo), no. 9(1984),   (P)
   pp. 26–28.
"Desejo," Fragmentos (Praia), no. 2(1988), p. 50.   (P)
"Dream of my homeland," English translation of "Sonhe pa nha terra,"   (P)
   and "Remembering," English translation of "Recordação," in M.M.
   Ellen, ed., Across the Atlantic. N. Dartmouth, Mass., 1988, pp. 31, 62.

PEDRO ALBERTO ANDRADE VIEIRA ("Canabrava"; born on Sal Island,
   1957)

"Desgraça," Terra Nova (Mindelo), no. 67(1980), p. 8.   (P)
"Morna & coladeira," ib., no. 88(1982), p. 5.   (P)
"Re-cor-dai, a noite de Natal," ib., no. 90(1983), p. 5.   (P)
"Sereia d'Santana," ib., no. 97(1983), p. 5.   (P)
"Nov horizont," ib., no. 98(1983), p. 4.   (P)
"Partida & regresso," Ponto & Vírgula (Mindelo), no. 7(1984), p. 26.   (P)
"A uma Maria qualquer," Fragmentos (Praia), no. 1(1987), p. 50.   (P)
"O vento dos tempos," "Drama de uma vida," "O pão é a razão de viver,"   (P)
   "Corpos & corpos no botequim a horas mortas," "Pão & suor," "In

articulo mortis," "Stória di nha vida," "Tambor & suor," "Re-cor-dai,
a noite de Natal," "A poesia está na rua," in *Aulil*. Sal Island,
Município, 1987, pp. 13–14, 21–23, 31–32, 38, 57–59, 66, 82, 86–87,
95–96, 113–114.
"Terra boa. . . de sol e vento," ib., pp. 91–92.   (C)
"Mistérios da noite," *Fragmentos* (Praia), no. 2(1988), pp. 38–39. (C)